YOGA AND MEDITATION

Also by James Hewitt

In the same series

YOGA POSTURES
YOGA AND VITALITY

TEACH YOURSELF YOGA
YOGA AND YOU

YOGA AND MEDITATION

by

JAMES HEWITT

BARRIE & JENKINS
COMMUNICA - EUROPA

First published in 1977 by
Barrie & Jenkins Limited
24 Highbury Crescent, London N5 1RX

ISBN 0 214 20468 5 Paperback

Typeset in Monotype Ehrhardt Series 453 & 573, by Jetset Typesetters Limited,
printed by Whitstable Litho.

Contents

List of Illustrations

I Why Meditate?

WHY MEDITATE?

The metaphysics, philosophy, and practices of Yoga have long fascinated a few Western scholars – but only in recent times have the practices been taken up with enthusiasm by many thousands of Europeans and Americans. In the great majority of cases, what they have taken up is an adaptation of Yogic disciplines to meet occidental needs, enhancing the quality of living. Most attention has been given to the postures (*asanas*), breath controls (*pranayama*), and relaxation exercises of Hatha Yoga, but a growing number of Westerners are now turning to the Yoga of Meditation for a variety of reasons, from its reasonable and valid use as a mental hygiene (all Yogic techniques are purificatory and promote tranquillity) to inner work towards Yoga's supreme goal of intuitive enlightenment. We should perhaps have written 'Goal', for the mystical experience sought is usually given a capitalization of its initial letter, whatever name it goes by – and there are many. The supreme goal of Yoga is the union ('Yoga' means 'union' or 'yoking') of the individual spirit with the universal spirit, the finding of one's essential nature (Self) beyond empirical ego, which has to be dissolved, and the seeing and experiencing of the ground of one's being. Thus such terms as Absolute, *Brahman*, God, Reality, Ultimate Reality, Cosmic Mind, Cosmic Consciousness, Universal Spirit, Over-soul, Over-self, Void, Buddha Nature. It, That – to name but a few – represent a goal for progress towards which body, breath, mind, and spirit are disciplined, refined, and perfected by psycho-physiological techniques, many of which provide great benefits for body and mind, in improved health, relaxation, tranquillity, and self-mastery, quite apart from the mystical end-goal for which they are a preparation.

MEDITATION AS MENTAL HYGIENE

Many levels of approach to Yogic meditation are possible. Readers may start out with one aim in mind, but switch to another level after a period of practice. One reason for meditating that is valid for every practitioner, whatever his viewpoint on Yoga's mystical frame of reference, is that meditation is a mental hygiene.

Such an approach is in no way unworthy of Yoga, for every discipline of Yoga has a purificatory nature. In this book's companion volume *Yoga and Vitality* we described techniques of posturing, breath regulation, relaxation, muscle and sexual controls, and hygienic practices, all of which traditionally serve the end of cleansing the organism. The psychological controls of Raja (Royal) Yoga are no less a purification than those of Hatha Yoga, but in Raja Yoga consciousness is worked upon directly, rather than indirectly through bloodstream, tissues, glands, and nervous system. Just as the techniques of the Yoga of Vitality cleanse the bloodstream, nerves, and body tissues, enhancing health and promoting poise and feelings of lightness, so do those of the Yoga of Meditation cleanse the mind, refine and clarify consciousness, lighten the spirit, and foster mental poise and equanimity. Meditation calms and tones the nervous system, relaxes, harmonizes psychic energies, recharges psychic batteries, and cultivates serenity.

HATHA YOGA AND RAJA YOGA

Some Raja Yogins dispense with the techniques of Hatha Yoga entirely, apart from the basic sitting postures for meditation, taking the view that if the state of consciousness is right, the body will be adequately cared for. This is an extreme view, though probably not without validity for the most advanced practitioners of Raja Yoga. The mainstream tradition sees the two approaches as inseparable, Hatha Yoga working on consciousness through bodily control and purification, and Raja Yoga working on the body through harmonizing the psychic energies and eliminating tensions and interference with the natural rhythm of nature.

Traditionally, Hatha Yoga is seen as a preparation for meditative Yoga. This is not to say that the former should be dropped in favour of the latter. Both should be practised, body influencing mind and mind influencing body to the heightened well-being of both. Swatmaram Swami, author of the *Hatha Yoga Pradipika* (which is translated 'a lamp [or light] on Hatha Yoga') says (59): 'There are many who are merely Hatha Yogins without the knowledge of Raja Yoga; I think them to be simple practitioners who do not get the fruit of their pains.' It may also be said that followers of the Yoga of Meditation are foolish if they aschew the aid of the exercises of the Yoga of Vitality.

THE QUIET MIND

Yoga meditation promotes psycho-physical poise and a quiet mind that protects against the stress of modern life, which destroys health and happiness, and is indeed a major killer in civilized society.

The newcomer to meditation receives a shock when he first sits down in a quiet place and turns his attention inwards. Our attention is normally turned outwards to cope with the challenges of the environment – but look within and you find that the mind is filled with the chatter of thought and the flashing of images; as rowdy as a cageful of mad monkeys, say some old Yoga texts. Yoga meditation sets out to reduce the clamour and the number of thoughts, to open up spaces between thoughts, to smooth out waves in the mind-stuff (*citta*).

Merely sitting still for a fifteen or twenty minute period each day – just sitting, letting thought flow and observing its flow – provides a mental hygiene of the kind we described. In fact, this is a meditative practice given pride of place by a leading school of Zen. But there are many other meditative methods, active and passive, to be described in the chapters to follow. The reader should experiment and select the method or methods best suited to his temperament, circumstances, and organism.

Meditation works upon the nervous system and the organism's physiological processes, and the results are extended beyond the duration of a daily session of contemplation to bring increased physical and psychical poise to life's daily activities. One experiences an inner sense of floating with the stream of life, with the Way or Course of Nature, which the Chinese call the Tao (pronounced 'dow').

William James, who made a still-unsurpassed study of the

psychology of religious experience early in this century, was impressed by the mental regeneration of a friend who had taken up Yoga practice, and wrote (28):

> The most venerable ascetic system, and the one whose results have the most voluminous experimental corrobation is undoubtedly the Yoga system in Hindustan. . . . The result claimed, and certainly in many cases accorded by impartial judges, is strength of character, personal power, unshakability of soul . . . a very gifted European friend of mine who, by persistently carrying out for several months its methods of fasting from food and sleep, its exercises in breathing and thought-concentration, and its fantastic posture gymnastics, seems to have succeeded in waking up deeper and deeper levels of will and moral and intellectual power in himself, and to have escaped from a decidedly menacing brain-condition of the 'circular' type, from which he had suffered for years. . . . A profound modification has unquestionably occurred in the running of his mental machinery. The gearing has changed, and his will is available otherwise than it was.'

Laboratory investigation confirms scientifically the subjective experience of lowered blood pressure, relaxed muscles and mind; and EEG tests on meditators show that their brain waves exhibit a slow pattern distinct from that of ordinary waking, hypnosis, or sleep.

THE MYSTICAL DIMENSION

It is but a short step from harmony with Nature or the Tao to meditating for reasons that are religious, or at any rate mystical. So far we have given reasons for meditating that are apart from the metaphysical and spiritual dimension. The word 'Yoga' has a mystical meaning as the supreme goal, as well as one representing the practices used to realize the goal.

Today in the West there is a widespread yearning for psychic Wholeness and a 'religious' feeling (in its broadest sense) that is eclectic and has no place for the doctrinal rigidities and dead dogmas of institutionalized religion. 'How does one live with religious emotion in the twentieth century?' asks Monica Furlong, in *Contemplating Now* (21). 'The longing for meaning, for wholeness, and for what the French philosopher Hubert Benoit calls "inner work" is common to everybody, but no one any longer, is sure of what the "work" consists of.'

Well, the Yoga of Meditation is the oldest form of 'inner work' still alive and in use, and it is one which many thousands of occidentals are finding puts them in touch with the springs of spiritual life. To quote Miss Furlong again (21):

> 'Most people are not aware of such a call, yet they may feel the strongest attraction to make some sense of the 'God-feeling' within them, and be overwhelmed by feelings of sickness, sadness, depression and despair if they suppress it because they disagree with conventional kinds of religious belief, or are afraid that others will think them mad or odd. If it is true that 'this is a society that represses transcendence' then they will find it painful to begin with to admit to being driven by such an improper longing, but if they will get past this stage they will discover that most people have a very good idea what they are talking about and are suppressing similar longings and experiences of their own.
>
> I believe that learning to admit transcendence may be one of the major undertakings of a man's life, perhaps the major undertaking, so that if it is ignored his personality may be stunted or destroyed. We are all contemplatives to a greater or lesser degree, and we all need, to the limit of our capacity, to admit the experience which we may, or may not, call God.'

Mystical experience transcends all religions and cultures, though each mystic tends to describe his experiences in the jargon of his particular religion and culture. But the sense of the unity of all things, the heart of the mystical experience, is not confined to followers of specific religions, and peak experiences of a spiritual nature can come unbidden to people who neither seek nor cultivate them.

Meditation offers the possibility of our opening up, as a flower to the sun, to the bright emotions of love and joy, even of ecstasy; of enriching immeasurably our relations with wives, husbands, children, parents, neighbours, and workmates – relationships based on I-Thou rather that I-It, in Martin Buber's well-known phrase.

GREATER SELF-MASTERY

Psychologists, neurologists, and doctors are now studying the psychological and physiological effects of Yoga practice and interpreting meditation in scientific language. Yoga, as an ever-developing living science, welcomes this investigation. Much to stimulate the intellect and imagination has resulted from such studies. There is the possibility, for example, that there are two distinct modes of consciousness, each related to one side of the brain. The left hemisphere controls language, verbal reasoning, and the time sense. The right hemisphere is responsible for intuition and 'spatial functions', including painting, sculpture, and dancing. Western culture, by this theory, has been left-hemisphere-orientated and Eastern culture has been right-hemisphere-orientated. This distinction will recur in a later chapter.

Laboratory tests have shown unusual patterns of brain wave production in meditators wired to EEG apparatus – waves distinct from those of the normal waking state, hypnosis, or sleep.

Meditators have demonstrated their ability to relax, to reduce their blood pressures, to slow down their heartbeats, to control, in fact, physiological functions thought to belong to the involuntary nervous system. This offers the possibility of regulating the health in ways not thought possible before. In addition to this, biofeedback equipment enables ordinary men and women to acquire control over physiological processes normally involuntary. After a short period of training in the use of the equipment, these subjects can display feats of self-mastery and conscious control over the involuntary nervous system of the kind demonstrated by exceptional Yogins.

MENTAL POWERS

The goal of acquiring exceptional mental powers (*siddhis*) is viewed with disfavour by respected Yoga masters, but it is a motivation for some people, and has been throughout Yoga's long history. Magic and the occult energies have always had a fascination for some sects of Indian Yoga and Taoist (Chinese) Yoga. Magic and the occult have also played a considerable role in Tantric Yoga, in particular that of Tibet.

That exceptional mental powers occur as a result of advanced Yoga meditation is claimed in all the major texts, including Patanjali's *Yoga Sutras*, but the main tradition holds that they are to be accepted lightly and not allowed to become distractions from the true goal of spiritual illumination.

WHAT IS MEDITATION?

At this point we should make clear what is meant by 'to meditate' in this work – and what 'to meditate' is not. It is neither to do what the dictionary defines as 'plan mentally, design', nor is it 'to muse, to think over', as is commonly assumed. There is a keen use of thought in Jnana Yoga, the way of the intellect, but most Yogas aim at a suspension of thought, a silencing of the mind's agitation.

Dictionary definitions of 'contemplation' bring us close to what is involved in oriental meditation. *The Concise Oxford Dictionary* defines 'contemplate' as 'gaze upon: view mentally'. The origins of the word are in the Latin *contemplum* or temple, an open space for observation. 'Contemplative' is defined as 'meditative, thoughtful; (of life in middle ages) given up to religious contemplation, opp. to active'. *Nuttall's Standard Dictionary* gives as one definition of contemplation, 'continued attention to a particular subject'.

Attention is the key. Meditation, as used in this book, is a general term applied to the methods of steadying, quieting, or opening the mind for purposes of altering states of consciousness. In the great religions its goal is a knowledge of the Absolute, personalized in Christianity and Islam, but impersonal in Vedantic Hinduism, Buddhism (a religion without a god), Zen, and Taoism. Esoteric and occult schools think more in terms of 'higher knowledge', 'heightened consciousness', or 'intuitive awareness'. The aim of meditation may also be, as shown above, at the less exalted (but valuable) level of relaxation and mental hygiene.

In terms of the Raja Yoga of Patanjali, meditation means sense withdrawal (*pratyahara*) and concentration (*dharana*), sustained into contemplation (*dhyana*), with the aim of triggering a superconscious state (*samadhi*), which is one of intuitive realization of the identity of the individual soul or spirit and the cosmic soul or spirit.

MANY YOGAS

The inclusion here and there in this work of meditative practices from sources outside Hindu Yoga warrants an explanation. *All* techniques used to achieve some kind of heightened or higher consciousness or intuitive enlightenment may be considered as

Yogas. One can therefore talk of Hindu Yoga, Buddhist Yoga, Sufist Yoga, Taoist Yoga, and so on. There is even an Eskimo Yoga, using techniques corresponding with those of Indian Yoga. There are also Yogas that combine Eastern and Western methods of self-mastery, such as the inner work for 'the harmonious development of man' taught by George Gurdjieff and his successors.

Sufism (Islam's mystical wing) and Christianity were both influenced by Indian Yogic methods, and Buddhism's whole *raison d'etre* is the meditation (*dhyana*) of its founder, an Indian prince. Buddhist meditative methods are pure Yoga. Buddhism was carried from India to China, where developed the direct method of Ch'an (meaning 'meditation'), which took root in Japan as Zen (again meaning 'meditation'). Tibetan Buddhism has a large content of Tantric Yoga practice. Finally, it may be said that, wherever they are found in the world, contemplative practices essentially follow the techniques of Indian Yoga. They all utilize in some manner the beam of attention. Attention again and again is the key that unlocks the door to altered states of consciousness and Self-realization.

II Yoga's Hindu and Mystical Setting

THE HISTORY OF YOGA

The practice of Yoga meditation has to be seen against the traditional backdrop of Hindu belief and culture. Though Yoga is not a religion, it *is* a system of psycho-physiological techniques that people can employ for spiritual unfoldment, and its history is linked with that of Hinduism, into which it was incorporated by the Brahmins, the priestly caste. And Yoga's whole *raison d'etre* is mystical, its ultimate aim being the experiencing of the Reality underlying all manifest forms. Therefore, to understand better Yoga's goals, methods, and terminology, we should have some acquaintance with its Hindu and mystical frame of reference.

Robert Linssen, the French Oriental scholar, says (37): 'Indian thought largely emanates from a mixture of two currents: yoga, established before the Vedic period, and Brahmanism, which belongs to the period of the *Vedas*, the *Upanishads*, and the *Vedanta*.' During the Mohenjo Daro excavations in the Indus basin, the John Marshall expedition discovered intact ceramics about five thousand years old on which were depicted Yogic meditative postures. Yoga thus pre-dates the main Vedic currents of Indian thought, which began about 1500-1000 BC with the *Rig Veda*, the *Sama Veda* and the *Yajur Veda*, followed by the *Atharva Veda* about 1000-800 BC, the *Brahmanas* about 800-600 BC, and the first *upanishads* about 800-500 BC. The six philosopical schools (*darshanas* or 'viewpoints') developed about 200 BC-500 AD.

The different forms of Yoga have played a major part in forming the spirit of modern India. Yoga is incorporated in Indian religion, in vernacular literature, and in folk-lore. Professor Masson-Oursel (37) calls Yoga a discipline of psycho-physiological behaviour that is the permanent basis of Indian culture.

Yoga's mental disciplines are, to varying degrees, part of the meditative methods of Buddhism, Taoism, Ch'an, and Zen. The words 'Ch'an' and 'Zen' both mean 'meditation'. Yogic techniques are also found in Sufism, and they had some influence on Christian mysticism.

HINDUISM

Hinduism is in several respects a unique religion. Unlike Chrisianity, Buddhism, or Islam, it had no founder and is not centred on the personality, teachings, and historical activities of a founder figure. It grew gradually over a period of five thousand years, during which time it absorbed and assimilated several religions and cultural movements in India. Without embarrassment or discomfort, it contains a great gallimaufry of religious, metaphysical, and philosophical ideas.

K. M. Sen (55) says that it is

> the recognition of 'many paths', each valid in itself but none alone complete, that gives to Hinduism its immense variety. The religious beliefs of different schools of Hindu thought vary and their religious practices also differ; there is in it monism, dualism, monotheism, polytheism, pantheism, and indeed Hinduism is a storehouse of all kinds of religious experiments.

For this reason Hinduism, throughout its long history, has been tolerant of all paths to spiritual truth, and has developed a remarkable capacity for absorbing disparate religious, metaphysical, and philosophical views. The multiplicity of viewpoints has been at the same time a strength and a weakness.

Hinduism is sometimes said to be a culture rather than a religion. K. M. Sen says that 'Hinduism is in fact a *dharma* rather than a religion in the restricted sense of the word.' *Dharma* is a difficult word to translate into English, for it has a cluster of meanings – 'way of life', 'civilization', and 'national consciousness' are three of them. Hinduism is a matter of conduct rather than of doctrinal belief. As Professor Radhakrishnan, in *The Hindu View of Life*, says (50): 'The theist and the atheist, the sceptic and the agnostic may all be Hindus if they accept the Hindu system of culture and life . . . what counts is conduct, not belief.'

'The attempt to translate it (Hinduism) into the verbal concepts and categorical structure of Western language leads to logical monstrosities,' writes Arthur Koestler, in *The Lotus and the Robot*, (34). Hinduism never had a St Paul or an Aquinas to tidy up its amorphous confusion. When the scholars get to work dissecting Hinduism, they end up with a multiplicity of parts labelled Vedism, Brahmanism, Saivism, Vaisnavism, and so on. But the Hindu, without straining, accepts all of the parts. He can incorporate the teachings of Buddha or Christ easily into his ideology – for he recognizes all paths to spiritual knowledge.

Hinduism is a national religion. The words 'Hindu' and 'India' share the same root – 'Indus.' Before the Islamic invasion, to be an Indian and to be a Hindu were one and the same thing. Hinduism is thought to have originated with the tribes of Aryans who migrated from Persia and the Eurasian steppes about 2000 BC., crossed the Hindu Kush, and settled in the valleys of the Indus and' the Ganges. Another wave of these nomads reached Syria and Egypt and founded the Hyskos empire about (1680-1580 BC). The Indo-European family of languages derives from the language the Aryans spoke, and includes most of the languages of Europe and a large part of south-west Asia. English and the other Germanic languages, the Romance languages derived from Latin, the Celtic, Greek, Slavonic, and Baltic languages all owe their origins to the speech of the Aryans. Sanskrit, the classical language of Hindu sacred literature and of Yogic philosophy, also derives from the Aryan language.

The polytheistic religion of the Aryans can be typified by the *Rig Veda*. Their gods personified the forces of nature: sun, fire, storm, and so on. They had both male and female deities. Their main method of worship was sacrifice in the open air. Some time between 800 and 500 BC Hindu polytheism gave way to monotheism.

Jainism and Buddhism emerged out of the complex Indian culture. Buddhism was strong for a time in India, reaching its peak during the third century BC. But Hinduism regained ascendancy and Buddhist masters and monks carried their religion to other lands. The meditative methods of Buddhism and Hinduism are closely related, and one leading school of Buddhism is called Yogacara. The Tantric Buddhism of Tibet, Nepal, and China incorporated many of the psycho-physiological techniques of Hindu Hatha Yoga. By the time of post-Buddhist Hinduism the main Yogas were all clearly established: Jnana, Karma, Bhakti, and so on.

THE HINDU GODS

The gods representing the single divine principle are numerous and of varying characters. The Hindu Trinity is composed of Siva, Vishnu, and the many-headed Brahma. Siva has a fierce character, needed to combat the demons; he is also a god of fertility, whose symbol is the phallus and whose symbolic animal is the bull. He is both a god of fertility and of destruction. The strongest Siva worship is found east of Benares. Vishnu has a milder character and is most worshipped west of Benares, where Bhakti (devotional) Hinduism is strong. He has many *avatars* or earthly incarnations, including the popular heroes Krishna and Prince Rama. Brahma, often confused with *Brahman* or Ultimate Reality, represents the divine power of creation. There are also Great Mother goddesses, such as the fearsome trio Durga, Kali, and Shakti.

CASTE

Since Vedic times each Hindu has been born into a caste, and each caste has had its rules and place in the Indian social system. The four main groupings are: i. *Brahmins:* the highest caste, the priests who alone could interpret the *vedas* and sacred writings. Today Brahmins are not always priests. ii. *Kshatriyas*: princes, warriors, and aristocrats. iii. *Vaisyas:* merchants, farmers, and professional people. iv. *Sudras:* servants and labourers.

The caste system may have originated before the Ayran invasion of the Indus Valley, but certainly the racial difference between the conquerors and the dark-skinned Dravidians contributed to its development. The fairer-skinned Aryans occupied the top castes, and the Indian labouring caste has tended to be dark-skinned. The Buddha was a Kshatriya by birth, but repudiated the caste system. There are many sub-castes. Each caste and sub-caste has its elaborate system of rules laying down which profession or employment a member should undertake, whom he should marry, what food he should eat, what clothing he should wear, what kind of house he should have, how it should be furnished, and so on.

It is to the credit of the drafters of the Indian constitution that there is no support in it for the caste system. It survives, but under mounting pressure. It remains strongest in south India. The complexity of modern urban living makes strict adherence to caste rules in cities impossible. Westerners are puzzled how caste has persisted, especially in the light of the lofty doctrine that the Self (*Atman*) of every man and woman is identical with the Over-self (*Brahman*).

STAGES OF LIFE (ASRAMAS)

Traditionally there are four stages or *asramas* laid down by the Brahmins for the life of the devout Hindu. They begin after childhood. i. The youthful period of discipline and education, during which the sacred writings are studied. ii. The period of the householder, the man occupied by his job, raising a family, and social responsibility. His duties should be performed in the spirit of Karma Yoga, and he may practise other Yogas. iii. The period of maturity, when his sons have grown up, married, and themselves become householders. Now he withdraws from family and social life, and takes instruction in spiritual development and Yoga at an *ashram*. iv. The final period, in which he becomes a wandering holy man, without property except for one robe, a staff, and a begging bowl. These aged mendicants are still a familiar sight in India.

The four-stage system has now been given a more modern look. For example, the Yoga schools (*ashrams*) are no longer crude huts with dried cow dung on the floor (as stipulated in some classic texts), but bright, clean, and attractive modern buildings in most cases.

The stages described above fit in with C. G. Jung's view that after middle age people develop a yearning, conscious or unconscious, for psychical Wholeness.

The final fourth stage of the devout Hindu's life is that of renunciation and non-attachment, in which he aims for *moksha* or *mukti* (Liberation). This concept is closely connected with two other Hindu ideas: *Karma* and Reincarnation.

KARMA

By the law of *karma* every human deed leaves a trace in the organism. We choose our actions and must be prepared to pay the price.

Each act shapes future action for good or ill. *Karma* should not be viewed as 'fate', as it popularly is in the West. A man takes responsibility for shaping his future life, or lives.

REINCARNATION

The concept of Rebirth is closely related to that of *karma*, for the *karmic* law of cause and effect extends through successive lives, according to Hindu belief, and hundreds, perhaps thousands, of lives may be needed to work off *karmic* impressions, a residue of which remain in even the enlightened man.

'Only in a long series of successive lives are the effects of our deeds and our actions undone,' writes Kovoor T. Behanan (5).

> We live now because of our past *karma* and for the same reason we shall live again. Life is thus an expiation of the deeds of the previous existence and as long as it is accompanied by action and deeds the necessity for further expiation makes rebirth inevitable.
>
> It is startling how a doctrine of rebirth like this, which can never be verified, has been accepted and believed as a solution for the riddle of existence. Cultured and illiterate alike find in it a just answer to the inequalities and sufferings of life. It inspires in its adherents a hope for the future coupled with submissive resignation in the face of present suffering. To say the least, the theory is, so far as the moral order is concerned, as logical as any other, which perhaps accounts for its acceptance. In its cardinal features the doctrine is found in the teachings of the ancient Greek philosopher, Pythagoras. Plato, too, believed in it.

MOKSHA (LIBERATION)

Moksha or *mukti* is release from *karma* and liberation from the cycle of rebirths. Buddhists use the term *nirvana* for this liberation. *Moksha* and *nirvana* sound negative states, and this view is reinforced by the use of the term 'Void'. But Hindus and Buddhists view them as fulfilments, as plentitudes, freedom, breaking of bonds, the opening of prison doors – fullness of being.

Moksha and *nirvana* are not annihilation, and we need not fear letting go our grip on the ego. All Yogas – Hindu, Buddhist, Sufist, and so on – share a common aim of dissolving the ego and realizing a higher Self. Swatmaram Swami, in the *Hatha Yoga Pradipika* ('a lamp [or light] on Hatha Yoga'), says (57): 'The Yogi in highest meditation is void within and void without like a pot in world space. He is also, like a pot in the ocean, full within and without.'

SACRED LITERATURE

Hinduism has no central founder figure: neither has it a supreme sacred book comparable in absolute authority with the Christian Bible or the Islamic Koran. However, certain works – principally the *Vedas*, the *upanishads*, and the *Bhagivad Gita* – are by Indian minds and hearts cherished as lofty expressions of Hindu wisdom. We have already pointed out how Hindusim accommodates a gallimaufry of concepts, many of which conflict. The same applies to Hindu sacred literature, in which conflicting ideas may be found within a single work.

Indian philosophy could be said to originate in the *vedas*, among the oldest of writings, though they are largely ritualistic, the main portion of each *veda* being taken up with the incantations (*mantras*) and hymns addressed to gods and goddesses, and the *Brahmanas*, written in prose, which deal with the rules and regulations for the performance of rites and sacrifices by the Brahmin priests. As appendages .to the *Brahmanas* there are the more philosophical *aranyakas*, whose closing passages are called *upanishads*, also known as *vedanta* (literally 'the end of the *veda*'). The word *veda* means 'knowledge' – compare the latin *videre*, 'to discern'. *Upanishad* derives from the root *sad*, which means 'to sit down'. *Upa* means 'near by', and *ni* means 'devotedly'. The whole word refers to the teachings received by the pupil sitting before a sage.

The *upanishads* educate and at the same time calm the spirit. Their monist thought, following on *vedic* polytheism, is poetical, lucid, and tranquil, But they not only criticize the earlier works to which they are appended – they mock them. The *upanishadic* sages were rebels who despised arid ritual and empty formulae. The *Chandogya Upanishad* contains a passage which compares the Brahmin priests to dogs marching in procession and chanting: '*Om!* Let us eat, *Om!* Let us drink, and so on!' OM (AUM) is the most sacred of all words to the Hindu.

The polytheism of the *Rig Veda* gave way to a search for unity within universal forms, and in the *upanishads*, with their teaching that *Atman* or Self equals *Brahman* or Cosmic Over-self, we find the purest Yogic philosophy. There are over two hundred *upanishads*, but ten or twelve are considered the most authoritative.

Few Westerners fail to appreciate, as poetry and as metaphysics, the beauty of the *upanishads*. The same may be said of the *Bhagavad Gita*, or 'Song of the Blessed Lord'. Both works have been translated several times into English and other European languages. The *Gita*, as it is popularly known, is part of the great epic called the *Mahabharata*. The Lord of the title is Krishna, a much-loved Indian deity, who in activities as an *avatar* or divine incarnation combines the qualities of a successful saint, warrior, poet, musician, and lover. The *Gita* takes the form of a discourse delivered by Krishna to Arjuna, the epic's hero, on the eve of a battle. Krishna instructs Arjuna in the way of duty and the ultimate goal of life. In doing so he expounds several Yogas.

The *Brahma Sutra*, written by Badarayana about the second century BC, sets out to explain the philosophy of the *upanishads*. The writer summarizes the views of earlier teachers, and refers to most of the leading systems of Indian thought. It is the third work in the threefold canon (*prasthanatraya*) on which the spiritual tradition of India is based (the first two works being the *upanishads* and the *Bhagavad Gita*).

BRAHMAN EQUALS ATMAN

One concept dominates the teaching of the *upanishads*, which express it again and again – the equation, *Brahman* equals *Atman*. The *Atman* is the Self, not the ego constructed principally by our parents, our teachers, and society. Yoga methods dissolve the empirical ego and permit the Self to be discovered. Self or *Atman* is then experienced as *Brahman*. *Brahman* is the divine principle 'in-forming' the universe, the essence and substratum of all things, all-pervading, the 'one without a second' (*ekamevadvitiyam*). *Brahman* is not God, if by God one means a personalized deity like the punishing and rewarding, wrathful and loving father-figure of Christianity; but the modern existentialist theologian's ground of being comes close to it. *Brahman* is the mystic One, and many labels are applied – though labelling the One is attempting the impossible.

'The most important step in the development of Indian philosophy was taken when the *Brahman*, the cosmic principle, and *Atman*, the psychic principle in man were looked upon as identical,' writes Kovoor T. Behanan (5). The identity of cosmic mind with our own pure consciousness is expressed in two sayings: 'that thou art' (*tat tvam asi*) and 'I am *Brahman*' (*aham Brahma asmi*). Dr Behanan says that this concept is 'a tacit assumption of mystics all over the world, irrespective of credal affiilations.' At this point Yoga becomes universal and transcends its Hindu setting. Mystics the world over believe in a unity behind the changing experiences and phemona of life, and that this substratum is contacted and known by looking within.

'This idea [*Brahman equals Atman*] alone secures to the *Upanishads* an importance reaching far beyond their land and clime,' writes P. Deussen in *Outlines of Indian Philosophy* (13). He goes on, 'for whatever means of unveiling the secrets of Nature a future time may discover, this idea will be true for ever, from this mankind will never depart. If the mystery of Nature is to be solved, the key of it can be found only there where alone Nature allows us an interior view of the world, that is in ourselves.'

MAYA

What prevents us seeing that our essence and Cosmic Mind are one? The Indian philospher replies: '*maya* (illusion) and *avidya* (ignorance.)'

Yoga techniques, of which there are a variety, each with a different emphasis of approach – intellectual, devotional, psychical, physiological, and so on – cut aside the veil of illusion and disperse the fog of ignorance that prevents the clear perception and experience 'I am *Brahman*'. Indian teaching makes an analogy between the world seen as illusion (*maya*) and a coil of rope mistaken for a snake. Move closer and you see that what you took to be a dangerous snake is but a coil of rope. There is then nothing to do but relax and laugh. So, too, when the veils of illusion and ignorance are penetrated, one perceives one's real nature as 'the one without a second'. The enlightenment and awakening triggers joy and bliss, and we laugh because our real nature was there all the time, though we had failed to look in the right direction. But a glance that way would have been sufficient. As T'sen T'sang put it: 'A difference of a tenth of an inch and the Heaven and earth are set apart.'

THE MYSTICAL EXPERIENCE

We have just described the mystical experience, essentially the same for mystics of all nationalities, cultures, and religions, though dressed by them in the conceptual and verbal clothing of the culture and tradition to which they belong. Such description is always futile. The mystical experience of intuitive awareness and inner illumination transcends linear verbal thought. In it duality is overcome, subject and object fuse: there are no longer perceiver, perceived, and perceiving as separate entities – all three fuse together to become a unity that belongs to the cosmos itself.

William James, in his *Varieties of Religious Experience* (29), a work still unsurpassed in this field for its breadth and penetration, says:

> This overcoming of the usual barriers between the individual and the Absolute is the great mystic achievement. In mystic states we become one with the Absolute and we become aware of our oneness. This is the everlasting and triumphant mystical tradition, hardly altered by differences of clime or creed. In Hindusim, in Neoplatoism, in Sufism, in Christian mysticism, in Whitmanism, we find the same recurring note, so that there is about mystical utterances an eternal unanimity which ought to make a critic stop and think.

III Yogic Philosophy

THE SIX SYSTEMS OF PHILOSOPHY

Yoga may be defined as mystical absorption. It is also a general name for the controls and techniques that perfect body, mind, and spirit so as to realize the mystical end-goal. Now we come to a third meaning. Yoga is one of the six systems of Indian philosophy (*darshanas*). *Darshana* means 'viewpoint' or 'vision', from the root *drs*, 'to see', 'to comprehend', 'to contemplate'.

The six schools of philosophy developed in the post-*upanishadic* period. For the theory behind its practice, Yoga borrows extensively from the Samkhya (or Sankhya) system, and the two names are often linked with a hyphen. The remaining four philosophies may also be paired, giving Samkha-Yoga, Mimansa-Vedanta, and Nyaya-Vaisesika.

Yoga differs from all the other systems in that it is not content, as they are, to expound metaphysical knowledge, but has devised and presented practical techniques whereby intellectual understanding can be reinforced by experiental knowing. Yoga says: 'Don't take our word for it Through psycho-physiological controls you can attain higher consciousness and experience on a level of Being the truth that will set you free.' This accounts for Yoga's great popularity and potency in Indian culture.

As all the Indian philosophies have the common aim of spiritual emancipation, it is thus possible for adherents of any school to borrow Yoga's practical techniques. This explains why leading Yoga masters may expound what is a predominantly Vedanta-Yoga teaching rather than the Samkhya-Yoga philosophy one might expect. But as all the systems have basically different approaches to metaphysical knowledge, in most respects they may be considered more complementary than contradictory.

Considering their age, these Indian philosophies are a remarkable achievement of human thought. Their texture is complex and dense. Count Hermann Keyserling, in writing his *Travel Diary of a Philosopher*, pointed out that Indian literature has more words for philosophical and religious thought than can be found in the Greek, Latin and German languages combined. We will here concisely outline the most important features of Yoga as a philosophy, particularly these most relevant to the practice of the Yoga of Meditation. Students of Yoga who wish to go deeper could not do better than start by reading the relevant chapters of Dr Behanan's *Yoga: A Scientific Evaluation*, which, though written in 1937, remains the clearest exposition for the general reader.

SAMKHYA YOGA

There is an old Indian saying: 'There is no knowledge equal to the Samkhya, and no power equal to the Yoga.' Samkhya is mainly a natural philosophy. Yoga takes from Samkhya its detailed account of the evolution of the known world and the nature of human consciousness. The leading Samkhya source text is Kapila's *Samkhya Sutras*, and the key work in the philosophy and practice of the Yoga of Meditation (Raja or Royal Yoga) is Patanjali's *Yoga Sutras*. *Sutras* are condensed statements – the word is usually translated as 'aphorisms'.

Richard von Garbe (22), a German oriental scholar, wrote that 'in Kapila's doctrine, for the first time in the history of the world, the complete independence and freedom of the human mind, its full confidence in its own powers, were exhibited.'

Samkhya and Yoga differ in two main respects. First, Samkhya is atheistical, but Yoga introduces – though awkwardly and weakly, it may be thought – a Supreme Being (*Isvara*), who stays aloof from human and worldly affairs, but acts as an inspiration. Second, Samkhya's approach to liberation is by way of metaphysical knowledge, intellectually accepted, whereas Yoga's approach is by way of psycho-physiological techniques and controls, though it uses Kapila's account of evolution, consciousness, the body-mind problem, and so on, as a theoretical support.

Samkhya explains the universe without seeing any need to introduce God. There is no anthopomorphized Creator. Kapila explained eternal evolution and dissolution in the universe in terms of *Purusha* (soul or spirit) and *prakriti* (basic substance), and the latter's evolutes. But Yoga, taking Samkhya's natural philosophy, added a Supreme Being, a liberated *Purusha*, who provides inspiration, but does not take an active role in human affairs. Thus God appears in Patanjali's *Sutras*, without fitting easily into the philosophical and metaphysical teaching of that work. Some scholars think that the appearance of *Isvara* in the *Sutras* was a later interpolation. Richard von Garbe says (22) of Patanjali's work: 'The passages which treat of God are unconnected with the other parts of the book – nay, even contradict the foundations of the system.'

VEDANTA

Most modern Yoga masters teach Yoga practice combined with the metaphysics of Vedanta: the '*Brahman equals Atman*' equation of the *upanishads;* the impersonal, all-pervading *Brahman* rather than a personal Creator, a concept which educated Indians find naive and unsophisticated. On this matter William James wrote (29):

> God as intimate soul and reason of the universe has always seemed to some people a more worthy conception than God as external creator. So conceived, he appeared to unify the world more perfectly, he made it less finite and mechanical, and in comparison with such a God an external creator seemed more like the product of a childish fancy. I have been told by Hindoos that the great obstacle to the spread of Christianity in their country is the puerility of our dogma of creation. It has not sweep and infinity enough to meet the requirements of even the illiterate natives of India.

Anta means 'end', and Vedanta is the knowledge found in the later *upanishadic* part of the *vedas* – *Brahman* ast he one Reality. Samkhya-Yoga holds to the doctrine of the purality of souls (*Purushas*), with *Isvara* (God) as a special *Purusha*. This clashes with the Vedanta *Brahman* concept, which is monist – *Brahman* is All, and each of us can say: 'I am *Brahman*.'

The best-known branch of Vedanta philosophy is Advaita Vedanta, founded by the brilliant Indian philosopher Sankaracharya, whose central tenet is non-duality.

Dr Behanan says (5) 'The vedanta has dominated the Hindu mind for so long that today most yogins have grafted the vedanta metaphysics to the yoga practice – *Brahman* alone is real. It is the adaptability of the system that makes yoga more a philosophy and a psychology than a religion.'

PURUSHA

We have Dr Behanan's assurance (5) that 'in its essential aspects the samkhya-yoga soul, called *purusha*, is not very different from the *Upanishadic Atman*.' However, the Samkhya Yoga doctrine of the plurality of souls (*Purushas*) marks a divergence from the monism of the *upanishads*, in which only *Brahman* is real.

Purusha is pure consciousness (*cit*), eternal, spaceless, passive, the Seer or Witness. It is the unchanging clear light against which the mind's thoughts and images becomes visible: not the images on the mental screen, but the projector's illumination. The relationship between *Buddhi* or Intelligence and *Purusha* is that the former reflects the latter.

Prakriti, the basic substance of the universe, serves *Purusha*. *Purusha* iniates cosmic evolution by coming into proximity with matter.

PRAKRITI

Dr Behanan (5) compares *upanishadic wisdom* with Samkhya *knowledge*. 'The wisdom of the *Upanishads* was, of course, the highest, but the *knowledge* of the samkhya had no equal because it was the boldest and most rational speculation in the field of natural philosophy.'

Samkhya means 'number'; it is the 'philosophy of number'. It probably received its name from its enumeration and classification of the twenty-five *tattwas* – the 'thatnesses' or categories of the known universe.

Samkhya Yoga teaches eternal alternating evolution and dissolution. Cosmic evolution is in the service of *Purusha* or Spirit, and proceeds from the subtle to the gross, from consciousness to gross atoms – the reverse of the customary direction of evolution as held by Western science.

The basis of all is *prakriti*, eternal and originally unmanifest.

Prakriti is often translated as 'Nature'. Dr Behanan (5) calls it 'primordial, undifferentiated matter' and Professor Wood (67) defines it as 'the basic substance or principle of the entire phenomenal or manifest world.'

The basic substance of things (*prakriti*) can be divided into three inherent qualities called *gunas*. These *tamas*, *rajas*, and *sattva* – or inertia, energy, and intelligence respectively. Alternative definitions of *sattva* are 'orderliness', 'purity', and 'illumination'. These three qualities or *gunas* combine to make up all the objects of Nature. They are both substance and energy. The predominance of a *guna* in a thing determined its essential nature.

Tamas represents mass, resistance, stability, solidity, and durability – though modern science tells us that all objects display ceaseless change – even the lamp-post that Dr Johnson kicked to disprove Bishop Berkeley's philosophical idealism. In the workings of the mind *tamas* is responsible for the stability of memory.

Rajas is the kinetic principle, responsible for the activity within the atom, and for change and motion everywhere in Nature. Within the mind it is responsible for the coming and going of thoughts and the ebb and flow of the emotions.

Sattva is the principle in Nature that makes for orderliness, that keeps the planets in their courses, designs the snow crystal's perfection, and regulates the involuntary functioning of the body. But *sattva* is found in its most characteristic element in the workings of consciousness. *Sattva* predominates in the 'mind-stuff', manifesting itself as intellect, will and feeling. It represents a pure and light quality, in contrast to the gross and heavy element in matter. But *sattva* is latent in heavy matter, just as *tamas* is latent in 'mind-stuff'. Energy (*rajas*) operates upon both *tanmas* and *sattva*.

STAGES OF COSMIC EVOLUTION

Prakriti's first evolute is *mahat*, *buddhi*, or Cosmic Consciousness, resulting from the three *gunas*, which were in dynamic equlibrium in primordial matter, being acted upon by *Purusha*. This is the plane of consciousness in which subject and object are fused, the goal for meditating minds in Yoga, Zen, Sufism, and other mystical traditions. *Buddhi* (intelligence) is passive at this stage.

In *mahat*, *sattva*, the basis of mental life, predominates. Thus, according to Samkhya-Yoga, the 'mind-stuff' originates immediately, reversing the customary scientific interpretation of evolution as a progression from inorganic to organic matter, and hence to whatever composes human consciousness. *Sattva*, being translucent, reflects spirit or *Purusha*. Dr Behanan provides an analogy (5): 'A piece of rock and a crystal are both composed of atoms, but the latter can reflect the rays of the sun while the former cannot. *Sattva*, as against the other two *gunas*, has that something in its nature which, although different from *purusha*, makes the reflection of the latter possible.'

The next modification is *ahamkara*, the 'I' – sense. It is produced by energy (*rajas*). This should not be confused with pure consciousness, which is *Purusha*.

The process of evolution now takes on three aspects, each dominated by a separate *guna*. From the *sattvic* aspect develop the senses of sight, hearing, smell, taste, and touch. Samakahya-Yoga adds a sixth sense – mind or *manas* in its faculty of co-ordinating. The *rajas* aspect produces the motor organs – hands, feet, speech organs, excretory organs, and generative organs. The *tamas* aspect is responsible for the five potentials (*tanmatras*) of matter, corresponding to the cognitive senses listed above – light, sound, smell, taste, and touch. There is a further evolution from the *tanmatras* into the five gross atoms – earth, water, fire, air, and ether

The above make up twenty-four categories or 'thatnesses' (*tattwas*). *Purusha* brings their total to twenty-five. The diagram will help make the Samkhya-Yoga account of cosmic evolution more clear.

THE TWENTY-FIVE CATEGORIES (*TATTWAS*)

1. *Purusha*
2. *Prakriti*, Basic Substance
3. *Mahat*, *buddhi*, Cosmic Consciousness
4. *Ahamkara*, 'I' – Sense

The Six Senses	The Five Motor Organs	The Five Potentials (*tanmatras*)
5. sight	11. hands	16. light
6. hearing	12. feet	17. sound
7. smell	13. speech organs	18. smell
8. taste	14. excretory organs	19. taste
9. touch	15. generative organs	20. touch
10. *manas* (mind as co-ordinating faculty)		
		The Five Atoms
		21. earth
		22. water
		23. fire
		24. air
		25. ether

YOGA METAPHYSICS

Metaphysics seeks to grasp with the intellect 'the totality of things', which was Hegel's description of the Absolute. It was once a major concern of Western philosophy, but became uncertain when the Logical Positivists declared that statements that cannot be scientifically verified are without meaning, including talk of the Absolute or God. 'Is metaphysics possible?' then became the subject of the debate.

But Yogic and Western metaphysics differ in that the former does not rely on intellectual acceptance of a theory, but says something like this: 'Sit quietly, breathe evenly, silence your mind's chatter – and you will see into your inner nature and enter the plane of Being.'

In this work, with its practical approach, the metaphysical bases of Yoga provide only a backdrop to its practice. The reader is free to question the validity of the backdrop's design. But whatever his (or her) views on speculative Yogic metaphysics and philosophy, there can be no doubt that practical benefits accrue on many levels from the practice of Yoga. These were described earlier, in the chapter entitled 'Why Meditate?'

And few readers will fail to agree with Kovoor T. Behanan, when he concludes his 'scientific evaluation' of Yoga by saying (5): 'As far as the metaphysical tenets of yoga are concerned, they are an audacious and poetic leap in the dark – worthy enough to occupy a spacious hall in the "Mansions of Philosophy" that the human mind has spun in its irrestible desire to explain the warp and woof of the unknown.'

IV Sitting for Meditation

SITTING FOR MEDITATION

This chapter is concerned with the pre-requirements for meditation, the two most important of which are a poised and stable sitting posture and the right attitude to take towards controlling the mind.

PLACE

The *Bhagavad Gita*, which calls itself a 'scripture of Yoga' and is the most translated work of world literature after the Bible, provides guidance in how to set about meditating. It says:

> 6.11. Having in a cleanly spot established a firm seat, neither too high nor too low, with cloth, skin and kusa grass thereon.

The room chosen for regular meditation should be clean and airy, and free from draughts and extremes of temperature, either hot or cold. The surroundings should be as pleasant and restful as possible for all the senses. Choose a place likely to be free from interruptions, either by people or the impingements of sense stimuli on the eyes, ears or skin. An outdoor place is sometimes suitable, but most meditators sit down to quieten the mind in bedrooms or other rooms in their homes.

A cushion will be a fully adequate substitute for the 'cloth, skin, and kusa grass' mentioned in the *Gita*. Place it on an even floor.

CLOTHING

Clothing should be light and comfortable. Remove the tie, collar, belt – anything which constricts or is likely to constrict. (No clothing at all should be worn when circumstances permit, but becoming chilled will not aid meditation.) Remove all objects from the pockets of trousers, shirts, and so on. Do not wear shoes or stockings.

CLEANLINESS

Bathe or sponge the whole body before sitting down to meditate; or wash the face and hands at least. Brush the teeth and rinse out the mouth with water. Empty the bladder, and the bowels too, if possible. Cleanliness and purification are an important part of Yoga practice.

EATING AND DRINKING

> 6,16. Yoga is not possible for him who eats too much, nor for him who does not eat at all, nor for him who is addicted to too much sleep, nor for him who is [ever] wakeful, O Arjuna.

The *Gita* here gives guidance for the eating and sleeping habits of a Yogi. A lesson can also be drawn in relation to sitting for meditation. If the stomach is full, respiration and circulation of the blood are impeded, and Yogins say that the movements of *pranic* energy currents are checked. Nor is an uncomfortably empty stomach desirable for a meditator, for it results in distracting sensations. Allow at least two hours to go by after a main meal before sitting down to meditate.

Overeating or undereating are alike detrimental to success in Yoga. A Yogic rule is that one should finish a meal feeling that a little more could have been taken. An old text put it like this: 'Half [the stomach] for food and condiments, the third [quarter] for water and the fourth should be reserved for free motion of air.'

SLEEP

Sleeping too much or too little is detrimental to the lucidity and alertness of mind required for meditation. Though by meditating in the Yogic manner one recharges mental batteries and touches deep levels of energy, the practice should not be used to refresh a fatigued mind. Meditation requires a clear and alert mind; a tired mind will be unable to sustain one-pointedness.

MODERATION

The Yogin is enjoined to show common sense and moderation in his habits of eating, drinking, sleeping, and daily exercise. Self-mortification and grim asceticism are not supported by the *Gita* or any of the main textual authorities.

> 6, 17. To him whose food and recreation are moderate, whose exertion in actions is moderate, whose sleep and waking are moderate, to him accrues Yoga which is destructive of pain.

POSTURE FOR MEDITATION

> 6, 13. Holding erect and still the body, head, and neck, firm, gazing on the tip of his nose, without looking around.

Descriptions of the possible Yogic postures or *asanas* for meditation are given in *Yoga Postures*. The most famous posture for meditation is the Lotus Posture, sometimes called the Buddha Pose. However, it is a difficult pose for the average Westerner, and may take many months to master. Much easier poses can be used. The essential factors are to sit keeping the back upright and to have the head and neck poised in line with the spine. Beginners may for a time utilize a wall or chair-back to provide support for the spine. In the main traditional postures the legs are crossed in some manner. The easiest Yoga posture is Easy Posture (*Sukhasana*) in which the legs are crossed tailor's fashion and the knees are kept as low as is comfortable. But if this proves difficult to sustain you can always sit on a straight-backed chair in the Egyptial Posture.

EGYPTIAN POSTURE

This way of sitting on a straight-backed chair resembles a pose often depicted in Egyptian sculpture. The feet and knees are kept together, and the soles of the feet are flat on the floor. The palm of the right hand rests flat on the top of the right thigh a little above the

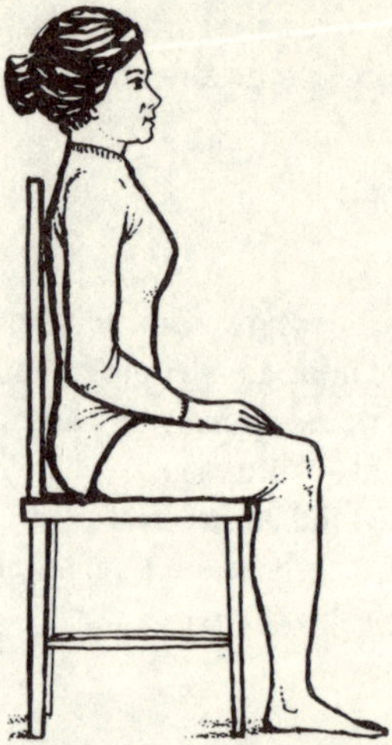

1 Egyptian Posture

knee, and the left palm is similarly placed above the left knee.

Maharishi Mahesh Yogi, the most successful *guru* in the West, does not insist on the cross-legged posture for his Transcendental Meditation, and says that sitting on a chair can be satisfactory so long as the back is kept erect. However, the unmatchable compactness and stability of the cross-legged Yogic postures will be apparent to anyone who takes the trouble to master at least one of them. The Easy Posture is not difficult, as its name reveals.

Lying on the back is not considered a suitable position for meditation because it causes drowsiness and dullness of mind. We shall see later that the mind should be in a normal state of wakefulness for meditation – neither dull nor very active.

EASY POSTURE (*SUSKHASANA*)

Sit on a cushion on the floor, cross the ankles, and lower the knees towards the floor as far as is comfortable. Keep the head, neck, and backbone in upright line. Rest the palm of the right hand on the right knee and the palm of the left hand on the left knee. Sometimes cross the right ankle over the left, and sometimes cross the left ankle over the right.

The knees will lower further as the weeks go by. When they rest easily on the floor it is time to move on to the Perfect Posture.

2 Easy Posture

Become accustomed to the Easy Posture by sitting in it while watching television, listening to records, feeding the baby, and so on. Remember that the body has to be forgotten in the tuning within of meditation; by practising sitting cross-legged at other times you can make the sitting posture comfortable and unobtrusive to the mind during meditation.

When Patanjali listed *asanas* or postures as the third of his eight limbs (*angas*) of Yoga, he was not primarily concerned with the numerous postures for good health that are found in Hatha Yoga, but with steady sitting postures for meditation. The most important thing is that the head, neck, and spine should be held poised easily in upright line. These essentials for sitting in meditation are aided by the practice of the Yoga of Posture, whose exercises and muscle controls strengthen the spine and back muscles, improve posture, and develop suppleness in the leg and hip joints.

PERFECT POSTURE (*SIDDHASANA*)

Siddha means 'adept'. This pose is so named because it is a favourite of 'perfected' Yogins. The right leg is bent at the knee, and by grasping the ankle, the right heel is pulled in against the pernieum, which is the soft flesh between the genitals and anus. The left leg is then folded and pulled back so that the left heel is against the pubic bone and the outer edge of the left foot, with the soles upturned, is

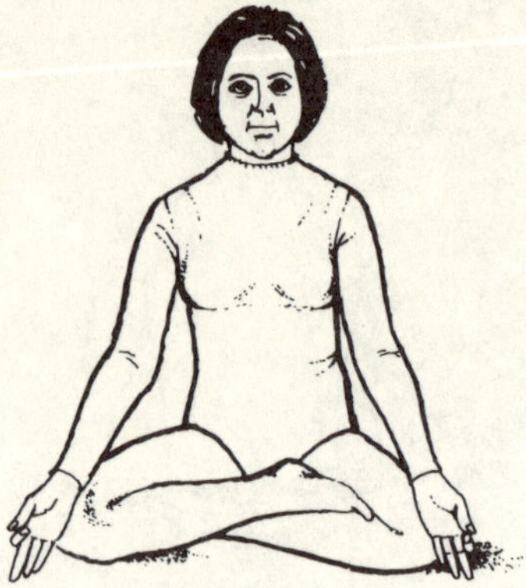

3 Perfect Posture

inserted in the fold between the calf and thigh of the right leg. Both knees are kept down on the floor. Place the right palm on the right knee and the left palm on the left knee, or clasp the hands loosely in the lap. Keep head, neck, and backbone in a straight vertical line. Sometimes reverse the roles of the legs so that the left heel is tucked in against the perineum and the right foot is pushed into the fold between the thigh and calf of the left leg.

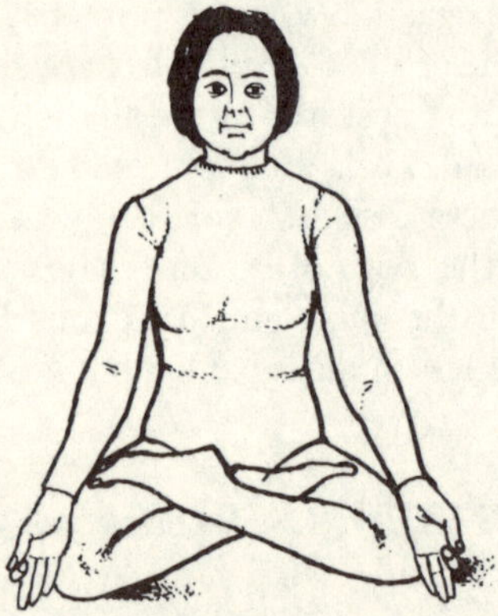

4 Lotus Posture

LOTUS POSTURE (*PADMASANA*)

In this famous pose, which occidentals find difficult, both feet are upturned on the thighs, right foot on left thigh, left foot on right thigh, each as high up the thigh as possible. Draw the feet up by pulling on the ankles. Here again the knees must be down firmly on the floor; if one is raised the pose will be unstable and lopsided. The hand positions may be as given for Perfect Posture – that is, on the knees or clasped limply in the lap.

Preparatory exercises for both Perfect and Lotus positions were given in *Yoga Postures*.

It is important to use for meditation a posture which is firm and in which the body is at ease. An old Chinese Buddhist text says: 'If the body is at ease, the Tao will prosper.'

Before leaving this section on posture for meditation, it is necessary to explain that when the *Gita* instructs the Yogin to gaze 'on the tip of his nose' this should not be done other than momentarily. Sankaracharya says (56): 'He is to gaze *as it were* on the tip of his nose. Here we have to understand the words "as it were": for the Lord [Krishna] means to prescribe, not the very act of "gazing on the tip of his nose", but the fixing of the eye-sight within (by withdrawing it from external objects); and this, of course, depends on the steadiness of mind.'

If the gaze is directed to the front of the nose the attention is drawn in and integrated. The eyes should then be closed and the gaze released. The brief focusing of the gaze has helped sense-withdrawal (*pratyahara*) and instantly induced a concentrated state of mind. Some texts instruct that the attention should focus on the navel or a little below it, which 'nails down' rising thoughts. The space between the eyebrows is another much-favoured spot for directing and fixing the attention.

BREATHING

Breathe quietly, through the nostrils, not the mouth. During meditation the breathing rate will slow down and establish an even rhythm between inhalation and exhalation. The breath controls described in detail in *Yoga and Vitality* will aid in calming the nervous system and stimulating the physiological processes that aid meditation.

Breath control (*pranayama*) is the fourth of Patanjali's eight limbs of Yoga. The Yoga system uniquely utilizes the influence of breathing on mental states: fast and jerky breathing excites the mind, but slow, smooth, and rhythmic breathing calms it.

RIGHT ATTITUDES

> 6, 12. Making the mind one-pointed, with the actions of the mind and the senses controlled, let him, seated there on the seat practise Yoga for the purification of the self.

'A normal state of mind is needed for starting meditation,' says Maharishi Mahesh Yogi (40).

> The mind should neither be dull nor very active. When it is dull, tending to sleepiness, it loses the capacity for experience. When it is very active, it remains in the field of gross experience, and, as it were, refuses to enter into the field of subtle experience, just as someone very active on the surface of the water does not sink.

One-pointedness of mind is the practical aim of the Yoga of Meditation. The attention rests steadily on one object until the knower, the known, and knowing become one in Enlightenment.

> 6, 10. Let the Yogin try constantly to keep the mind steady, remaining in seclusion, alone, with the mind and body controlled, free from desire, and having no possessions.

In these three lines from the *Gita* the conditions for successful Yoga meditation are concisely presented.

Quietness, privacy, and a secluded place in or outside of the home are needed for practice. The likelihood of disturbance should be reduced to a minimum. The abrupt ringing of a telephone bell in the room in which you meditate can have an unpleasantly jarring effect on the nervous system, so stay well away from telephones, or leave the receiver off the hook. 'During meditation the mind engages itself in the deeper levels of the thought-process', says Maharishi Mahesh Yogi (40): 'if it is disturbed and suddenly made to come out into the gross levels of sensory perception, it will experience a great contrast between the subtle and the gross fields of perception. This sudden contrast will damage the mind's serenity and will upset the nervous system.'

Meditation should be practised alone, as the presence of one or more other persons in the room will prove a distraction and prevent relaxation. One is all too conscious of their proximity and breathing presence.

The body should be stable and without movement, the spine kept upright and the head and neck in line with it. Suitable postures were described earlier in this chapter.

The mind has to be quietened and then kept steady. Such control is virtually effortless in correct performance. Concentration, after its initial gentle impulse, like a singer launching a soft head note, sustains itself and becomes free-flowing in the higher contemplative stages. One should not be trying to do this or that during meditation, for each intention is a distraction and a cause of tension and strain.

Professor Wood says (67):

> Before you meditate you choose your subject or object of meditation, and there is then an act of will in which you tell your mind to keep to that subject and not to wander away from it.
>
> This concentration on the chosen subject then goes by itself, and you need not think of it. If you have decided to walk in a certain direction the legs go on walking; you need not think of this act of will at every stage. An act of will goes on operating until another act of will changes it. Similarly, the act of concentration is still there while the meditation is going on, though it has been forgotten – 'subconscious' or 'unconscious' is the new word for this, though really it is now a habit, an act of the mind lapsed into inert form or motion.

'Free from desire' Maharishi Mahesh Yogi translates as 'expecting nothing'. A longing for Self-knowledge is necessary for the fully-committed Yogin, but no expectations should be entertained when he sits down to meditate. To expect any particular psychological or spiritual experience during meditation is certain either to block its attainment or to produce results that are ego-projections and not truly of the Self. The expectations are based on the known, which is the conditioned past; whereas Self-realization is a timeless and unconditioned experience, transcendent, on another plane of consciousness, hence totally new.

'Having no possessions,' says the *Gita*. Interpretations of this vary from the literal way of renunciation of the *sannyasi* to the state of going into meditation empty-handed, that is, without mental baggage, objects of thought or emotions that have to be grasped or recorded by consciousness.

During the stage of sense-withdrawal (*pratyahara*) one 'gives up' the external sense objects or possessions to turn the attention inward and sink down to subtler layers of consciousness. The meditating Yogin has also to be free from the tensions created by the tug-of-war between polar opposites and the interplay of the three *gunas*. Thus, the *Bhagavad Gita* states:

> 2, 45. The Vedas treat of the triad of the *gunas*. Be, O Arjuna, free from the triad of the *gunas*, free from pairs, free from acquisition and

preservation, ever remaining in the *Sattva*]Goodness], and self-possessed.

But the major possession the Yogin must release is the ego, which dissolves during meditation.

COMING OUT OF MEDITATION

Instruction in this is omitted in many manuals, but it is important for the health of the nervous system that the meditator should return gradually from the subtle to gross levels of activity. A Chinese Buddhist text cited by Charles Luk (38) puts it:

> Entry and exit should be both orderly for then
> The states of coarse and fine do not impair each other.
> This is like a horse that's tamed
> At your will to stay or go.

At the conclusion of meditation, sit quietly for a few minutes before opening the eyes. Blink the eyes a few times as though releasing energy from them and clearing them. Unfold the legs and stretch them out straight along the floor. Stretch the legs away from the body for a few seconds, at the same time stretching both arms straight up from the shoulders so that the fingertips reach up towards the ceiling. Lower the arms. Take two or three deep abdominal breaths while sitting on the floor. Massage the legs with the hands for about a minute. Then stand up. Never jump up immediately meditation has ended.

HOW LONG SHOULD MEDITATION LAST?

It has been found that sessions of meditation lasting twenty to thirty minutes once or twice a day are most effective.

V Patanjali's Royal (Raja) Yoga

THE YOGA SUTRAS

'In (the) basic literature of Yoga, the *Yoga-Sutras* of Patanjali stand out as the most authoritative and useful book,' says I. K. Taimini (60), one of the best modern commentators on this work. 'In its 196 *Sutras* the author has condensed the essential philosophy and technique of Yoga in a manner which is a marvel of condensed and systematic exposition.'

Patanjali divides his famous work into four sections. Section 1 answers the question 'What is Yoga?', and since the goal of mind-stilling by Raja Yoga is the higher state of consciousness called *samadhi*, this section is called *Samadhi Pada*. *Pada* means 'part of a book'.

The first part of Section 2 investigates the causes of suffering (*klesa*), and the second part describes the external practices (*bahir-anga*) of Raja Yoga. The *sadhaka* (seeker or aspirant) is here shown how to make a start with practice (*sadhana*) whereby he can achieve his goals. Section 2 is called *Sadhana Pada*.

The first part of Section 3 deals with the internal practices (*antaranga*) leading the aspirant to *samadhi*. The second part describes the psychic powers (*siddhis*) that may be acquired. The section is called *Vibhuti Pada*. *Vibhuti* means 'divine power'.

Section 4 deals with the philosophy and metaphysics of Yoga and the nature of mind and consciousness. The practical aim behind the theory is emancipation or spiritual freedom (*kaivalya*). Hence this final section is called *Kaivalya Pada*.

THE *SUTRA* METHOD OF EXPOSITION

Indian philosophical works employ the *sutra* method of exposition –

terse, close-knit, packed so densely with meaning that a commentary on each *sutra* is necessary.

Sutra means 'thread'. The English word 'suture' and its Latin root *sutura* are linked etymologically with the Sanskrit *sutra*. The condensed statements are strung together to outline a philosophy. *Sutra* has the secondary meaning 'aphorism'. 'Just as a thread binds together a number of beads in a rosary, in the same way the underlying continuity of idea binds together in outlining the essential aspects of a subject,' says Mr Taimini (60).

> The most important characteristics of this method are utmost condensation consistent with clear exposition of all essential aspects and continuity of the underlying theme in spite of the apparent discontinuity of the ideas presented. The latter characteristic is worth noting because the effort to discover the hidden 'thread' of reasoning beneath the apparently unconnected ideas very often provides the clue to the meaning of many *Sutras*. It should be remembered that this method of exposition was prevalent at a time when printing was unknown and most of the important treatises had to be memorised by the student. Hence the necessity of condensation to the utmost limit. Nothing essential was, of course, left out, but everything with which the student was expected to be familiar or which he could easily infer from the context was ruthlessly cut out.

This makes for difficulty for the modern student of Yoga confronted by the printed text: the meaning has to be mined from the dense prose. Fortunately, commentaries are usually available. To quote Mr Taimini again (60):

> We have to remember that in a treatise like the *Yoga-Sutras*, behind many a word there is a whole pattern of thought of which the word is a mere symbol. To understand the true significance of the *Sutras* we must be thoroughly familiar with these patterns. . . . Luckily for the earnest student, Yoga has always been a living Science in the East and it has had an unbroken succession of living experts who continually verify by their own experiments and experiences the basic truths of this Science. This has helped not only to keep the traditions of Yogic culture alive and pure, but to maintain the meanings of the technical words used in this Science in a fairly exact and clearly defined form.

In India the seeker has through the centuries been able to receive explanations of Patanjali's condensed exposition of the Royal Path from the mouths of the 'living experts'. Today we can obtain the necessary clarification from the printed word. Many distinguished exponents of the Yoga of Meditation have translated the *Sutras* into English and provided commentaries. Without such expansions and elucidations of the highly-contracted aphorisms we would have little chance of getting at the real meaning of the text. A difficulty is that there are no exact English equivalents for many of the Sanksrit terms; translators go as near as they can, and often cannot do other than retain the use of the original Sanskrit word.

We are using here the translation of Manilal Nabhubhai Dvivedi (15), still one of the clearest. Quotation marks are used to denote quotations from his explanatory notes, based on the famous commentary of Vyasa and others. His translation I have changed in one brief but important respect. For his 'contemplation – absorption – trance' I substitute 'concentration – contemplation – *samadhi*', the terms I have used throughout this book for the final three stages of meditation.

SECTION 1 OF THE *YOGA SUTRAS*: STILLING THE MIND

1, 1. Now, an exposition of Yoga [is to be made].

Here, in the very first *sutra*, it is clear that Patanjali is not the originator of Yoga, which goes back many centuries before Patanjali's birth. But Patanjali is about to expound its teaching and methods. The 'Father of Yoga', as Patanjali is called, is its first systematizer. Little is known of him, and his identity is disputed by scholars. He is thought to have lived and written the *Yoga Sutras* in the third and second centuries BC.

1,2. Yoga is the suppression of the transformations of the thinking principle.

Or it could be called checking the mind's modifications. Here Raja Yoga is summed up in only a few words. Its aim and practice is stilling the mind. The Sanskrit original has only four words: *Yogas citta-vritti-nirodha. Citta* is the mind-stuff, *vritti* (literally 'whirlpool') the mind's movement, and *nirodhah* means 'restraint'.

This Yoga is achieved by meditation that it is not thinking about something, but the quietening of thought, reducing the waves until the surface of the mind is calm and pellucid so that the white light of pure consciousness (*Purusha*) can shine in all its clarity. Dvivedi says, 'It should be distinctly borne in mind that the thinking principle is not the *Atman*, the *Purusha*, who is the source of all consciousness and knowledge. The suppression of the transformations of the thinking principle does not, therefore, mean that the Yogin is enjoined to become nil, which certainly is impossible.'

Citta manifests itself when consciousness is acted upon by matter. Its modifications can be reduced to one, as in *sabija samadhi* or *samadhi* 'with seed'. But the ultimate aim is to inhibit all transformations, in *nirbija samadhi*. The *jivatma* or individual soul then frees itself from its entanglement in matter (*prakriti*), the substance of the manifest world, and finds itself joined with *paramatma* or universal soul.

1,3. Then the seer abides in himself.

'When all the *vrittis* or transformations of the thinking principle are suppressed, there remains only the never-changing eternal seer, *Purusha*, in perfect *sattva* [purity], being only the perceiver. The ultimate fact of consciousness is itself and nothing else. This unalloyed bliss is the proper state of the highest Yoga called *Nirbija Samadhi*,' says Dvivedi.

The third *sutra* tells us what happens when the mind's movements are inhibited. The Seer is *drashta* or *drashtri*, the Witness or Looker. The meditator knows his essential nature. This, in short, is Self-realization. We are talking about the Self that is beyond the empirical ego; the latter is the public and private self mainly constructed by parents and society. The pure Self, our essential nature, is there all the time waiting to be uncovered. There is a profound mystery here. For we have already reached our goal if we but knew it. The Yogi works through Time to reach a goal which is the discovery that at the core of his being he was on the plane of the Timeless all along.

1, 4. But otherwise [he] becomes assimilated with transformations.

We should endeavour not to be caught up in the mind's agitation and movement, which prevents us knowing our real nature. The Buddhists call it 'Buddha nature' or 'Buddha mind', because it was this the Buddha uncovered when he meditated beneath a *bodhi* tree.

1, 5. The transformations are five fold, and painful or not-painful.

Even the pleasurable states of mind are disruptive. The discerning Yogin notes that desire for pleasure holds the seeds of pain. The next *sutra* lists the five transformations of the mind.

1, 6. [They are] right knowledge, wrong knowledge, fancy, sleep and memory.

The following five *sutras* describe these transformations:

1, 7. Right knowledge [is] direct cognition or inference or testimony.

1, 8. Wrong knowledge is false conception of a thing whose real form does not correspond to that conception.

'A post mistaken for a man,' says Dvivedi. Or a coiled rope mistaken for a snake.

1, 9. Fancy is the notion called into being by mere words, having nothing to answer to it in reality.

1, 10. That transformation which has nothing for its basis is sleep.

Sleep is a transformation, but *samadhi* is 'pure cessation of all transformations'.

1, 11. Memory is the not-allowing a thing cognised to escape.

1, 12. Its suppression is secured by application and non-attachment.

'Its' refers to transformations of the thinking principle. Non-attachment is called *vairagya*. Application means meditation. 'That which attracts the mind and makes it assume various forms as passions, emotions, sensations, etc., is nothing but *raga*, attachment; and *vairagya*, therefore, is . . . the absence of all attachment,' says Dvivedi.

1, 13. Application is the effort towards the state.

Dvivedi comments that '*Sthiti* or "state" is that state in which the thinking principle, as it were, stands, unmoved and unmodified, like the jet of a lamp in a place not exposed to the wind. The steady, sustained effort to attain this *Sthiti* is called application.'

1, 14. It becomes a position of firmness, being practised for a long time, without intermission, and with perfect devotion.

The point is that the mind comes at an advanced stage to a position in which, though apparently performing the ordinary functions of life, it is really at rest.'

1, 15. The consciousness of having mastered [every desire] in the case of one who does not thirst for objects perceptible or scriptural, is non-attachment.

Dvivedi comments that 'it is only when the mind reaches this condition of freedom from attachment, that true knowledge begins to dawn upon it, as right reflection in a mirror cleared of dirt.' Non-attachment should not be equated (though it often is) with feelings of indifference or coldness.

1, 16. That is the highest, wherein, from being the *Purusha*, there is entire cessation of any, the least, desire for the *Gunas*.

Purusha and the *gunas* were dealt with in an earlier chapter. *Purusha* is pure consciousness, spirit, or soul. The *gunas* are the three inherent qualities of *Prakriti*, which is primordial matter. They are *tamas* or inertia, *rajas* or activity, and *sattva*, which may be translated as rhythm, orderliness, or purity. 'This kind of *vairagya* is called *para* or the highest, as distinguished from the former which is only *apara* or lower,' says the commentary.

SECTION 1 OF THE *YOGA SUTRAS*: *SAMADHI*

Patanjali now goes on to describe *samadhi*, the goal of meditation. The practical work of stilling the mind to trigger this superconscious state is left until Sections 2 and 3. *Samadhi* is higher consciousness, the final stage of meditation. It has itself several stages or qualities, progressively finer. In Yogic meditation the attention drops like a pebble towards the sea- or river-bed of consciousness. A better simile, perhaps, would be produced by reversing the movement: a cork released from the sea- or river-bed and floating upwards to break the surface and meet air and sun.

In dealing with the stages of *samadhi* we are on very subtle psychological territory in which the distinction is made (1, 17 and 1, 18) between *samprajnata samadhi* and *asamprajnata samadhi.*

> 1, 17. Conscious [*samprajnata samadhi*] is that which is attended by argumentation, deliberation, joy, and the sense of being.

'Though the mind is free from transformations, still it is conscious of that which it identifies itself with, and hence this *Samadhi* is called conscious (*Samprajnata*),' says the commentary.

> 1, 18 The other is that which consists only of *Samskaras*, being brought on by the practice of the cause of complete suspension.

This is *asamprajnata samadhi*. The prefix *a* means 'not'. *Samskaras* are mental impressions traced by past experiences. *Pra* means 'higher', and *jna* means 'knowledge'. *Prajna* is variously translated as 'intelligence', 'wisdom', 'consciousness', and 'higher consciousness'.

I.K. Taimini says that *Prajna* is 'the higher consciousness working through the mind in all its stages'. He makes a distinction between the *samprajnata samadhi* and *asamprajnata samadhi* and the *sabjia samadhi* and *nirbija saamdhi* (*samadhi* 'with seed' and 'without seed', respectively) described by Patanjali towards the end of Section 1. Other commentators use the two sets of terms interchangeably. The difference for Mr Taimini is that he sees the first pair as alternating stages, and the final pair as the culmination of a process which he likens to an aeroplane passing in and out of cloud and finally emerging from the last cloud in the sky into clear air and light, which is consciousness of *Purusha*. This is achieved by breaking through progressively subtler vehicles and planes of consciousness. 'The recession of consciousness towards its center is thus not a steady and uninterrupted sinking into greater and greater depths but consists in this alternate outward and inward movement of consciousness at each barrier separating two planes,' (60) he says.

In the Transcendental Meditation taught by Maharishi Mahesh Yogi progress is made similarly by a succession of 'drops' into consciousness, which the Maharishi calls (40) 'turning the attention inwards towards the subtler levels of a thought until the mind transcends the experience of the subtlest state of the thought and arrives at the source of the thought'.

Dr Behanan (5) defines *samprajnata samadhi* as 'the stage of trance-contemplation in which the subject is conscious of the object of concentration,' and *asamprajnata samadhi* as 'the stage of trance- contemplation in which the subject is not conscious of the object of concentration.' Professor Wood describes the former as 'the kind of *samadhi* which has an objective *bhumi*' (ground or object of meditation and the latter as 'the superior kind of *samadhi*, in which the contemplation has no objective ground.'

Conscious (*samprajnata samadhi*) can be divided into four stages: *savitarka*, *nirvitarka*, *savicara*, and *nirvicara*. Here, Dr Behanan (5) gives the clearest account.

> Since *samadhi* is the last of the right stages and the goal towards which all efforts are directed, it is important to understand the nature of the yogin's experiences in this condition. Even here several grades are said to exist and the one quality which characterizes them all is the relative or total loss of subject-object awareness. That state in which the mind is one with the object (*artha*), together with the concept (*jnana*) and the name (*sabda*), called *savitarka*, is the lowest kind of *samadhi*. The object remains gross because it is identified with concept and name. In short, the associations formed in our waking life still persist.
>
> The next stage of *samadhi*, *nirvitarka*, is a grade higher than the above, in that the associations of name and concept are dropped off. The object is just the object without predicate relations. In the *savicara prajna*, the grossness of the object is no longer felt; its place is taken by the subtle constituents of matter (*tanmatras*). Perception, if one may call it such, is determinate because the *tanmatras* are subject to time,

space and casuality. In the fourth kind of *samadhi*, *nirvicara*, the *tanmatras* are finally dispossessed of the conceptual notions of time, etc.

These four stages are also called conscious-*samadhi* (*samprajnata-samadhi*), because there is, though only vaguely, a union between the subject and the object; the object is, so to say, still there. The *buddhi* continues to function as long as the object remains and the feeling of personality, accompanied by deliberation (*vitarka*), reflection (*vicara*), and joy (*ananda*), persists.

But the yogin's aim is to surpass the *citta* stage entirely: This condition is reached in the *superconscious-samadhi* (*asamprajnata-samadhi*), *Prakriti* (nature), through *citta*, does not bind the *purusha* any more, the sense of personality and the resultant joy are no longer experienced. The ultimate truth dawns on the yogin and the *purusha* abides in itself.

The stages of *samadhi*, which should not be identified with the unconsciousness of dreamless sleep or coma, are described by Patanjali later in Section 1:

1, 41. In the case of one the transformations of whose mind have been annihilated, there is entire identity with, and complete absorption in, the cogniser, the cognition, and the cognised, like a transparent jewel.

Meditator, the object, and the process of contemplation have fused.

1, 42. The argumentative condition [of the concentrated mind] is that which is mixed with thoughts of word, meaning and understanding.

The commentary says: ' This and the following *Sutra* refer to the *Sthula* or gross division of *Samprajnara Samadhi*. . . . When the mind apprehends a word and meditates upon its meaning and form, as also upon the understanding of either . . . it is called *Savitarka Samadhi* we are still holding in mind the name (*sabda*) and the normal conceptual associations.'

1, 43. Non-argumentative is that in which the meaning alone is present as if quite unlike itself, or memory being dissolved.

This is *nirvitarka samadhi*, the next grade up, in which word and understanding have been dropped.

1, 44. By these, the deliberative and non-deliberative having reference to the subtle elements are also explained.

The 'subtle elements' are the *tanmatras*.

1, 45. The province of the subtle ends with the indissoluble.

1, 46. These constitute seeded-meditation.

'Inasmuch as there is consciousness in this kind of *Samadhi* it is called seeded, for there is the seed which, on waking, may grow into various distractions from the condition of *Samadhi*'.

1, 47. The purity of the non-deliberative being reached, internal contentment follows.

'The last stage of *Samadhi* develops a sense of complete intellectuality, or complete absorption in the soul. . . . This is called *Adhyatmaprasada*. The qualities of *rajas* and *tamas* being entirely annihilated, so to speak, and *sattva* alone remaining . . . it is possible to experience the bliss consequent upon true recognition of the *Purusha*,' says the commentary.

1, 48. The intellect is there truth-bearing.

1, 49. Its subject is different from that of revelation and inference, for it refers to particulars.

1, 50. The impression thereof stands in the way of other impressions.

Dvivedi comments: 'We know that the last truth impressed on the mind is none other than blissful cognition of the *Purusha*. The mind ceases to transform itself into anything besides this impression.'

1, 51. The prevention of that even, leads to the prevention of all, and thus to meditation without seed.

Even the impression of having uncovered the *Purusha* is a seed (*bijas*). When even this fades away, *samadhi* with seed (*sabija*) gives way to *samadhi* without seed (*nirbija*), in which there is only pure consciousness'

Swami Vivekananda (64) describes the two stages with characteristic eloquence:

You remember that our goal is to perceive the Soul itself. We cannot perceive the Soul because it has got mingled up with nature, with the mind, with the body. The ignorant man thinks his body is the Soul. The learned man thinks his mind is the Soul; but both of them are mistaken. What makes the Soul get mingled up with all this? Different waves in the *Citta* rise and cover the Soul; we only see a little reflection of the Soul through these waves. So, if the wave is one of anger, we see the Soul as angry; 'I am angry,' one says. If it is one of love, we see ourselves reflected in that wave, and say we are loving. If that wave is one of weakness, and the Soul is reflected in it, we think we are weak. These various ideas come from these impressions, these *Samskaras* covering the Soul. The real nature of the Soul is not perceived as long as there is one single wave in the lake of the *Citta;* this real nature will never be perceived until all the waves have subsided; so, first, Patanjali teaches us the meaning of these waves; secondly, the best way to repress them; and thirdly, how to make one wave so strong as to suppress all other waves, fire eating fire as it were. When only one remains, it will be easy to suppress that also; and when that is gone, this *samadhi* or concentration is called seedless. It leaves nothing, and the Soul is manifested just as It is, in Its own glory.

Soul is of course *Purusha*. Later (in his *Raja Yoga*) (64) Vivekananda says:

> in this first state of *samadhi* (*samadhi* with seed) the modifications of the mind have been controlled, but not perfectly, because if they were, there would be no modification. If there is a modification which impels the mind to rush out through the senses, and the Yogi tries to control it, that very control itself will be a modification. One wave will be checked by another wave, so it will not be real *samadhi*, in which all the waves subside, as control itself will be a wave. Yet this lower *samadhi* is very much nearer to the higher *samadhi* than when the mind comes bubbling out.

A similar distinction is made in Zen Buddhism, where you have he stages of 'present-heart' (*ushin*) and no-heart' (*mushin*), heart here meaning consciousness. As an old Zen poem puts it: 'Being mindful of not-thinking is thinking nevertheless. O that I were now beyond thinking and non-thinking.' This sums up the difficulty and the final stage of Yogic meditation when concentration sustained into contemplation moves beyond thinking and non-thinking into *samadhi*.

SECTIONS 2 AND 3 OF THE *YOGA SUTRAS* THE EIGHT LIMBS OF YOGA

Having described the goal of Yoga meditation in Section 1, Patanjali turns in Section 2 to the disciplines that bring it about. He describes eight limbs (*angas*) making up the eightfold path of Raja Yoga. Raja means 'king'. The stages of this Royal Way are:

i. Abstinences (*yamas*)
ii. Observances (*niyamas*)
iii. Postures (*asanas*)
iv. Breath control (*pranayama*)
v Sense withdrawal (*pratyahara*)
vi Concentration (*dharana*)
vii. Contemplation (*dhyana*)
viii. Self-realization (*samadhi*)

The first two limbs are rules of conduct, ethical disciplines that ensure the Yogin is approaching the serious business of Self-realization in a suitable frame of mind. On an ethical plane they provide the purification that is essential preparatory training in Yoga.

There is a sense, however, in which Patanjali is here putting effect before cause and the cart, as it were, before the horse. Yogic morality reaches its full flowering in the Self-realized person. The same thing is true of the Eastern 'ways of liberation' in general. In Zen Buddhism, for instance, Christians are perplexed to find little or nothing in the way of ethical do's and don'ts. This is because the Zen masters know that the Zen experience, attained through meditation and other disciplines, will transform the personality of the aspriant, who will then, naturally, as a fully-realized human being, become compassionate, loving, calm, joyous, honest, truthful, and so on. Patanjali, too, was probably aware of the difficulties of being ethical by an effort of will on a lower plane of consciousness than the advanced Yogin can achieve, but felt that the attempt would do some good in creating a right attitude in the neophyte and in refining thought and emotion to some extent.

Stages 3 to 8 follow in natural order. One sits steadily in a Yogic posture (*asana*) of meditation which holds the back erect. One breathes quietly and evenly (*pranayama*). One withdraws the senses from their external objects and turns the attention inwards (*pratyahara*). An object of concentration is then held steadily by the mind (*dharana*), sustained into the free-flowing attention that is contemplation (*dhyana*). The final stage of Self-realization (*samadhi*) was dealt with in the last section; in this we will examine the preceding seven limbs.

The Five Abstinences (*Yamas*)

2, 30. Forbearance consists in abstaining from killing, falsehood, theft, incontinence, and greediness.

These five moral qualities go much deeper than just not-doing, and can be expressed as positives instead of negatives: non-violence, truthfulness, non-stealing, continence, and non-covetousness.

Non-violence (*ahimsa*) is not just avoiding killing, violence, and injury, but means also a positive compassion for all sentient creatures. It means avoiding anger and violent thoughts, and being gentle of mind. Where there is violence there is usually fear behind it. The practices of Yoga make for non-fear (*abhaya*) and for non-anger (*akrodha*).

Non-violence was the favourite precept of Mahatma Gandhi, who said of it:

> *Ahimsa* is not merely a negative state of harmlessness but it is a positive state of love, of doing good even to the evil-doer. But it does not mean meek submission to the will of the evil-doer: it means the putting of one's whole soul against his will. Working under this law of our being, it is possible for a single individual to defy the whole might of an unjust empire, to save his honour, his religion, his soul, and lay the foundation for that empire's fall or its regeneration.

In Indian folk-lore many stories are told of wild animals becoming gentle in the presence of a Yogi. Patanjali says: 'Near him in whom non-violence has fully taken root, all beings renounce enmity.'

Truthfulness (*satya*) has a deeper meaning than not telling lies. It means that our attitude to others should be marked by sincerity, integrity, and authenticity, to use a term loved by existentialists. There is also the deeper dimension expressed in the saying: 'Truth is God, God is Truth.'

Non-stealing (*asteya*) extends beyond physical objects to the psychological sphere – taking undeserved credit, for example.

Continence (*brahmacharya*) refers at one level to the austerity expected of the Hindu undertaking advanced Yoga practice. His *guru* commands chastity because of respect for the sexual energies which can be harnessed for spiritual ends. Sensual excitement would waste energy and distract the mind from its concentration and goals. Chastity is not, however, expected of the married 'householder Yogin', but continence would apply in a wider dimension of non-attachment to sensual pleasures – which does not mean trying not to enjoy a walk in pleasant surroundings or a cool drink on a hot day, but an attitude of not clinging to pleasures and not craving for their repetition. Think of a mirror, which receives but does not grasp.

Non-possessiveness (*aparigraha*) means not the absence of all possessions, but not clinging to them or craving unnecessary things. At the same time the Yogin is expected to reduce his possessions to a reasonable simplicity. This rule counters the Western mania for accumulating wealth and possessions, both seen as marks of prestige and identified with success in life. The Yogin has a very different concept of what constitutes the main goals of life.

The Five Observances (*Niyamas*)

2, 32. Observances consist in purity, contentment, mortification, study, and resignation to *Isvara*.

I prefer 'austerity' to 'mortification' in translating the third observance.

Purity (*saucha*) means both bodily and moral purification. Purification is much in evidence in Yogic practice. The breath controls, postures, hygenic processes, and dietary rules described in *Yoga and Vitality* all contribute to psychophysical purity, whereby body and mind are prepared for the progressive refinement of consciousness that is the Yoga of Meditation. Yogins are instructed to change the quality of their body cells by eating *sattvic* foods, and *sattva* is the *guna* which predominates in pure consciousness. Internal (ethical) purity is obtained by obeying the abstinences and observances.

Contentment (*santosha*) is cultivation of calmness and equanimity of mind. In this the immobile postures (*asanas*) and smooth, rhythmic breath controls (*pranayama*) are helpful. All the Yogic disciplines foster contentment and those qualities of character that so impressed William James in persons who had been practising Yoga for some time. Peace of mind comes, the Yoga masters say, when body and mind are kept pure. Yogins should be cheerful and uncomplaining – *tush*, the root from which *santosha* comes, means 'to be pleased'.

Austerity (*tapas*) refers to strength of character and to resolute pursuit of Yoga's goal of union of Self (*Atman*) and *Brahman*. The word *tapas* means purification by burning, which is often mistaken as self-mortification. This observance sometimes leads to fasting, a meagre diet, and other forms of asceticism. A moderate austerity trains the will and develops body and mind for the highest Yogic practice, but the *Bhagavad Gita* and the most respected Yoga masters warn against excessive asceticism and self-mortification.

In discourse 17, 5–6 of the *Gita* Lord Krishna says: 'Those men who practise terrific austerities (*ghara tapas*) . . . weakening all the elements in the body – fools they are – and Me who dwell in the body within; know thou these to be of demoniac resolves.'

Study (*svadhyaya*) includes reading the *upanishads*, the *Bhagavad Gita*, and the most highly-regarded literature of Yoga, and deep reflection on what is read. It also includes self-study, the stripping away of the 'not-I' selves described in the chapter on Jnana Yoga.

Resignation to *Isvara* (*Isvara Pranidhana*) is resignation to God, *Brahman*, That, It, Tao, or whatever title you wish to give the

Absolute. Nature, if you wish, which we are *of* and not just *in*. The observance can be taken as advice to let go, to stop clinging to the ego – a source of frustration, dissatisfaction, and tension – and to trust in the Self that is at the centre of wholeness of being. The ego thinks it is in charge and has an inflated concept of its own importance. Modern psychology has revealed to us the great regions of the psyche below the surface of consciousness, and C. G. Jung used the term Self over and above the ego for the organizer and integrator of the total psyche, of which the conscious part in which the ego operates is but a small part.

Isvara, the Supreme Being, is probably a later interpolation into Patanjali's *Yoga Sutras*, in which he sits uneasily as a model *Purusha*, an inspiration, and a recipient of devotion. The ego is melted by the fire of devotion (Bhakti Yoga), just as in Jnana Yoga it is whittled away by the well-honed intellect and in Raja Yoga dissolved by stilling the mind's agitation and modifications. In Christian language *Isvara pranidhana* is 'Not my will but Thy Will be done', 'Love God and do what you like', and losing your soul to find it. In Taoist language it is floating with the flow of life and Nature, the Tao.

The differing functions of the two aspects of Yogic ethical training are cogently summed up by I. K. Taimini (60): 'The practices included in *Yama* are, in a general way, moral and prohibitive while those in *Niyama* are disciplinal and constructive. The former aim at laying the ethical foundation of the Yogic life and latter at organizing the life of the *Sadhaka* for the highly strenuous Yogic discipline which is to follow.'

Postures (*Asanas*)

2, 46. Posture is that which is steady and easy.

The *asanas* in Raja Yoga are the seated meditative postures, whereas in Hatha Yoga the whole organism receives attention from a wide range of posturing, improving suppleness and flexibility, toning the nervous system and the glands, purifying the bloodstream and firming and strengthening the muscles, in a system unrivalled in its completeness and effectiveness for these purposes. In *Yoga Postures* over four hundred *asanas* are described.

Patanjali has here in mind only a few of the most stable sitting postures. The aim is to keep the body steady and the back straight, the chin held level and the head poised easily in line with the spine. This stage was described earlier in the chapter entitled 'Sitting for Meditation'.

The aim of meditative posture is not to focus attention on the body, but, on the contrary, to enable the meditator to forget about the body and to give his total attention to quietening the mind. Hence Patanjali continues:

2, 47. By mild effort and meditation on the endless.

To make sense, this *sutra* has to be joined with 2, 46. Thus: 'By poised effort and meditation on the infinite posture is steady and easy.'

Patanjali goes on to say that by mastering posture the Yogin is made free from assaults from the pairs of opposites. These are both bodily and mental: heat and cold is an example of the former, and joy and sorrow of the latter.

Breath Control (*Pranayama*)

2, 49. This being [accomplished], *pranayama* [follows] – the cutting off of the course of inspiration and expiration [of the breath].

This should not be taken literally. Suspension of breathing (*kumbhaka*) is a part of *pranayama*, as discussed and described in the large section given to Yogic breath regulation in *Yoga and Vitality*, and of the arousal of *kundalini* energy, but as far as meditation is concerned what is required is reducing the breathing to such smoothness and quietness that it is made as unobtrusive as the immobile and 'invisible' body.

Another feature prominent in Hatha Yoga thinking should also be pointed out. *Prana* is the life force, considered to be potent in the air we breathe. It is also the connecting link between matter and mind. I. K. Taimini (60) writes: '*Prana*, which exists on all the planes of manifestation, is the connecting link between matter and energy on the one hand and consciousness and mind on the other. Consciousness expressing itself through the mind cannot come into touch with matter and function through it without the intermediate presence of *Prana*.' Swami Vivekananda, a much earlier interpreter of Yoga to the West, put it (64): 'In this body of ours the breath motion is the "silken thread"; by laying hold of and learning to control it we grasp the pack thread of the nerve currents, and from these the stout twine of our thoughts, and lastly the rope of *Prana*, controlling which we reach freedom.'

Pranayama prepares the mind for meditation. It conduces to calming the mind-stuff (*citta*). The word itself indicates that it is restraint (*yama*) of *prana*, the life-force. Negative and positive *pranic* currents in the body are equalized and channelled in Hatha Yoga practice. Patanjali says that *pranayama* produces two positive results:

2, 52. Thence is destroyed the covering of light.

This does not mean that *Purusha* is uncovered – otherwise what need would there be for the remaining four stages? It is a reference to the '*tattvic lights*', the luminosity of the energy channels of the subtle body (*see* the chapter on Kundalini Yoga). That *Purusha* is not referred to is revealed by the following *sutra*:

2, 53. The mind becomes fit for concentration.

Pranayama, in common with the preceding stages, prepares the mind for concentration (*dharana*), contemplation (*dhyana*), and Self-realization (*samadhi*), which are the internal meditative techniques whereby the light of *Purusha* really is uncovered.

But first there is the initial process of turning inwards, called *pratyahara*.

Sense Withdrawal (*Pratyahara*)

2, 54. Sense-withdrawal is, as it were, the imitating by the senses of the thinking principle, by withdrawing themselves from their objects.

2, 55. There follows the greatest mastery over the senses.

Vivekananda (64) is clearer here: '2, 54. When the senses have withdrawn from their objects and transmuted themselves into the modes of consciousness, this is called "the Withdrawal", *Pratyahara*.' And the *Vishnu Purana* expands this a little: 'The adept in yoga gives himself up to "Withdrawal" and stops the traffic of the senses with their objects which are word, sight, etc., to which they invariably attached. He then makes his senses work for his Consciousness and the ever-agitated senses are controlled. No yogi can achieve the aim of yoga without controlling the senses.'

Two groups of sense-distractions have already been removed – those resulting from poor posture and from uneven breathing. We did this by making the body posture stable and at ease, and by regulating the breathing so that it flows smoothly and rhythmically.

Pratyahara is the initial process of turning the attention inwards, of inhibiting the reception of the bombardment by a myriad sense impressions to which we are at every moment subjected. This withdrawal of attention from external objects affects all the senses. Unless an object before one is being used for visual attention, the eyes should be closed. The sense responses of the skin, ears, nose, and tongue should also be closed down, as though by turning down the volume of a radio – though the analogy applies to only one sense, whereas all the senses should be shutting down to some degree in *pratyahara*. The sensations of sight, touch, hearing, smell, and taste are quelled. This requires practice, but as the days go by you will become more proficient in shutting out the external world.

A considerable amount of inhibition of external stimuli goes on automatically – otherwise our nervous systems would be so overloaded that they would collapse and suffer a total shut-down. A kind of inbuilt filtering valve has evolved which lets through to consciousness only those sense stimuli that are of interest and value to us. The function of the filtering valve is to preserve the individual and the human species as a whole. However, though this filtering goes on continually, unless you have already had experience of meditation in the Eastern style you will find it strange at first to withdraw into yourself as completely as you do in *Pratyahara*.

Now one problem immediately faced in Yoga meditation is that when we turn the attention inwards, having drawn it back from what is going on externally, we discover the unaccustomed world of what is going on *internally* – strange internal movements to do with physiological processes, little tensions and itchings, gurgles in the stomach, and so on. And, strangest of all, we find that our heads seem filled with unruly thoughts – some old Yoga texts refer to a cage full of excited monkeys. We have to learn to reduce and quieten these turbulent thoughts, which parade through the mind, dispute, and play, quite without invitation. Fortunately, we have the aid of a powerful technique in this work of stilling the mind's turbulence. It is Yogic concentration or *dharana*.

Concentration (*Dharana*)

Patanjali ends Section 2 of the *Yoga Sutras* with sense-withdrawal (*pratyahara*), and opens Section 3, called *Vibhuti Pada* (*vibhuti* means 'divine power'), with concentration (dharana). In fact, the first three *sutras* of Section 3 summarize concisely the nature of the final three stages of meditation in Raja Yoga.

3, 1. Concentration is the fixing of the mind on something.

It is best if the object selected for concentration is something fixed and unchanging – or at least appears to be, for science tells us that everything is in a state of movement and change. It may be a rose, a candle flame, the space between the eyebrows, a piece of broken glass, a tree on the horizon, or one of a million or more other objects. It may be a diagram drawn for the purpose of meditation (a *yantra*); or, if we employ the ears instead of the eyes to focus attention, it may be a voiced word or phrase held to have special meaning in this respect (a *mantra*), which may be spoken inwardly rather than aloud. It is possible for other senses – touch, for example – to provide the means whereby the field of consciousness can be narrowed. One can also narrow thought to a single thought.

In early training a small fixed object a few feet away, on which the gaze can rest, makes a good focus for concentration. After a few weeks, the eyes can be closed and the object held before the minds' eye.

Whatever the object chosen, the beam of attention should finally be held unwavering. If the mind wanders from its limited field of attention, it should be gently brought back, coaxed rather than dragged.

An analogy may be made with the spotlight which picks out, for the audience's attention, the movements of performers on a theatre stage. The stage is the area of the spotlight's beam of attention, and over this limited range it is free to roam.

We must keep the beam of our attention within a small area. Eventually the quality of the flow of attention changes and concentration gives way to a higher stage – contemplation (*dhyana*).

Contemplation (*Dhyana*)

3, 2. The unity of the mind with it is contemplation

'It' is the object of concentration. 'Absorption or *dhyana* is the entire fixing of the mind on the object thought of, to the extent of making it one with it. In fact the mind should, at the time, be conscious only of itself and the object,' says Drivedi.

Now the spotlight has stopped its slight movement up and down and from side to side and fixes unwavering on one point. If one sits immobile, quietly breathing, retracts the senses, and concentrates the mind on a restricted field, eventually the attention may be held steady without distraction or interruption. This is the stage of contemplation or *dhyana*, the penultimate of Patanjali's eight limbs of Yoga. A state of mental poise is sustained in an effortless flow. Now the meditator is close to breaking through to a new mode of consciousness. There is a change of quality from gross to subtle.

Self-realization (*samadhi*)

3, 3. The same, when conscious only of the object, as if unconscious of itself, is *samadhi*.

That is, the first stage of *samadhi:* consciousness, with seed. In the advanced stage of *samadhi* without seed, the meditator, the thing meditated upon, and the process of meditation are merged and become one, and consciousness is fully integrated.

3, 4. The three together constitute *Samyama*.

Samyama is the name given to the final three stages of meditation – *dharana*, *dhyana*, and *samadhi* – when practised successively with one and the same object.

3, 7. The three are more intimate than the others.

The internal stages of concentration, contemplation, and Self-realization are more intimate than the external stages that go before.

3, 8. Even it is foreign to the unconscious.

Even *samyama* is preparatory to seedless *samadhi*.

YOGIC METHODS OF MEDITATION

The techniques of Yoga meditation are more varied than those of the other esoteric psychologies. They may incorporate difficult and possibly dangerous psycho-physiological controls, as in Kundalini Yoga. They may require mastery over breath and muscle, as in Hatha Yoga. They may harness the energy of the libido, utilizing sex either directly or indirectly as a way to mystical experience, as in Tantric Yoga. They may be powerfully imaginative, as in Tibetan Yoga. They may make use of the vibratory power of human speech, as in Mantra Yoga, or the magico-occult power of design and form, as in Yantra Yoga. When the power of analytical reason is used to cut away layer upon layer of 'not-I' material that has accrued from parental and social conditioning to uncover the pure naked Self, then that is Jnana Yoga. There is concentration of the heart, of devotion, in Bhakti Yoga, and of action, work, and service in Karma Yoga. Patanjali's Raja Yoga, the 'Royal Way', emphasizes 'one-pointing' the mind and stilling thought. Some techniques are given in other chapters, and a few helpful concentrative methods will be described here.

Claudio Naranjo, in his study of contemplative exercises among the traditional disciplines (46), distinguishes between two types of meditation: 'concentrative' and 'opening-up'. The 'opening-up' method is mostly found in use in Buddhist schools. Yoga mainly utilizes concentrative exercises, and Patanjali's famous treatise, as we have seen, teaches that awareness is to be focused on a fixed point and the mind made steady. This is called concentration or *dharana*.

VI Techniques of Concentrative Meditation

CONCENTRATION (*DHARANA*)

Concentration (*dharana*) is the only one of the last three stages of Patanjali's Raja Yoga that comes under any measure of conscious control, and that, as was explained in describing the right attitude for meditation in the chapter on sitting for meditation, need only extend to the initial impulse that focuses the attention on the chosen spot. We may compare this with the impulses with which a great singer launches a note, which is then sustained and supported by the stream of breath and the diaphragm and some other body muscles. Or, to use different anologies, we may think of the skater's glide over the ice or the divers' leap from the springboard. The deeper stages of contemplation and Self- realization come to us by a kind of grace, provided the right quality of attention has been put into flow. They are not something that can be performed or willed. Start thinking 'I will do this' or 'I will do that' and you are right back where you started from, with thought, a buzzing active mind.

Concentration is preceded by sense-withdrawal (*pratyahara*). As a tortoise might withdraw its head into its shell, so you pull in the attention from external sense objects. Internal sounds and sensations take the place of external stimuli – such unfamiliar stimuli as itchings, tinglings, audible gurglings, the thump-thump of the beating heart, the passage of air in the nostrils and trachea. From these stimuli, too, you should withdraw.

The technique of *pratyahara* is as well known to the Christian mystic as to the Hindu Yogin. This is how Meister Eckhart (26) describes it:

The best and utmost of attainment in this life is to remain still and let

God act and speak in thee. When the powers have all been withdrawn from their bodily forms and functions, then is this word spoken. Thus he says: 'In the midst of the silence the secret word was spoken to me.' The more completely thou art able to in-draw thy faculties and to forget those things and their images which thou hast taken in, the more, that is to say, thou forgettest the creature, the nearer thou art to this and the more susceptible thou art to it.

Here the soul is scattered abroad among her powers and dissipated in the act of each: the power of seeing is in the eye, the power of hearing in the ear, the power of tasting in the tongue, and her powers are accordingly enfeebled in their interior work, scattered forces being imperfect. It follows that for her interior work to be effective, she must call in all her powers, recollecting them out of external things to one interior act.

To achieve the interior act one must assemble all one's powers as it were into one corner of one's soul, where, secreted from images and forms, one is able to work. In this silence, this quiet, the Word is heard.

In concentrative meditation the attention is fixed on one thing. If the beam chases after a sound or a thought, bring it back gently to rest on the meditation-object. When unbidden thoughts appear, check the kind of chain reaction, based on association, that could lead to several minutes of involuntary reverie. It can be appreciated that concentrative meditation is valuable training on a practical level, bringing a steady flow of attention to bear on work and life's activities in general. The mental faculty of concentration strengthens with practice. 'Genius is concentration,' Schiller said.

Dharana is restricting the attention to one point. It is concentration without tension. No clenching of fists, no biting of the lower lip, no knitting of the brow. The meditating Yogi should give the appearance of relaxed serenity. Yet he is giving all of himself to concentrative meditation – a whole person wholly attending. There is no thought of results. We have already discussed the right attitude to take for meditation in the preceding chapter.

In popular usage concentration means applying discursive reasoning to a chosen subject, excluding all irrelevant thoughts and painstakingly working with relevant thoughts. The field of attention becomes a small circle, but within that circle thought is busily engaged. Yogic concentration (*dharana*) is a very different matter, for it reduces a stream of thought to one thought, the object of attention, and there holds it unwavering. The object of attention is unimportant, and may be the most trivial of things. It is not that the single thought-track in the mind-stuff (*citta*) is so important that all other thoughts must be kept away, but that the method of holding a single percept in the mind is being used to still thought entirely. When sustained effortlessly, like a great singer's soft head-note floating on the breath, that single furrow across the mind's calm fades away like the grin on the face of the Cheshire cat in *Alice in Wonderland*. At a press conference in London I heard Maharishi Mahesh Yogi describe the technique as 'using a thorn to remove a thorn from one's flesh.'

Some writers on Yoga give preliminary exercises in which the meditator thinks about all aspects of the meditation object until he has exhausted all possible lines of thought about it. He then goes on to hold the mind steady. Thinking about and around a subject is the common Western concept of concentration – we do quite enough of it, and my view is that even the beginner should go direct to holding the attention steady, which is *dharana* proper.

Dr Kovoor T. Behanan, who undertook training in India with a famous teacher in order to make a scientific evaluation of Yoga, says (5):

> Another road open to the yogin to achieve his special goal is that of concentration, where attention is focused on a point. If a flower is chosen as the object of concentration, there is no consideration of its size, weight, or any other qualities whatsoever; it is mentally reduced to a point and kept before the mind as a mere idea. Any thought about the qualities or relations of objects only leads to a perpetual succession of ideas and this is precisely what the yogin wants to avoid. However barren this kind of focusing of the attention may seem, yogins claim that one-pointed concentration is dynamic enough to reach deeper levels of consciousness.'

STEADY GAZE MEDITATION

Trataka or gazing steadily at an object is one of the six purifying processes of Hatha Yoga, having the purpose of 'clearing the vision'. As a cleansing exercise the gaze is prolonged, without staring, but also without blinking, until the eyes begin to water. The eyes do not move and the gaze remains fixed on one point. Clairvoyance is one of the psychic powers said to result from the practice. Here, however, we are concerned with fixed gazing as a technique of of meditation and not as a hygiene for the eyes – though such meditation can be looked upon as a hygiene for the mind.

In visual concentrative meditation one should not gaze until the eyes water or become sore. Blink naturally when necessary, and as soon as the eyes tire close them and hold the image of the concentration-object before the mind's eye. Later you will have the ability to produce it at will by visualization.

A small object is preferable to a large one, though a small part of a larger object may be selected and, of course, large objects become small objects to the gaze when they are at a distance. A leaf on a tree may be the focus of attention, or the tree itself if it is on a distant horizon. Out of doors, the concentration-object may be a tulip or a daisy, a stone, a pebble, a clod, a piece of broken bottle – anything on on which the gaze can be fixed. Indoors, it may be an apple, a rose in a vase, the vase itself, a cross, a crust of bread, or a leaf on a bush in the garden visible beyond the window of the room you are meditating in. A picture may provide numerous points of interest, one of which should be selected. Hindus sometimes concentrate on a picture of a revered *guru*, saint, or diety. When gazing at a portrait, it is customary to focus the gaze on the space between the eyebrows or on the person depicted. A steady candle flame in a darkened room is sometimes suggested, both for *trataka* and for concentrative meditation. It is an apt choice, for four reasons. First, in the *Gita* we find:

> 6,19 'As a lamp in a sheltered spot does not flicker', — this has been thought, as the simile of a Yogin of subdued thought, practising Yoga in the Self.

Second, light is associated with mystical enlightenment. Third, the eyes are drawn to a bright point. Fourth, the bright image is easily retained as an after-image when the eyes are closed.

For some or all of the reasons just given, bright objects – a silver coin, the glint of sunlight on water or rock – have a strong appeal for many meditators. The seventeenth-century Christian mystic Jacob Boehme achieved enlightenment on gazing upon his cobbler's crystal as it reflected bright sunlight.

But points on which to focus the gaze are for all practical purposes limitless – and (again for practical purposes) the concentration-object can be as mundane as an old bath plug or a rusty can. However, it is understandable that for regular use meditators often select a religous symbol or an object that has either intrinsic beauty or associations with tranquillity.

There are obvious advantages in focusing on an object that is available at any time: hence the frequent mention in classic texts of tip of the nose, the space between the eyebrows (for the inner gaze), and the navel. However, in commenting on verse 13 of discourse 6 of the *Bhagavad Gita* in the chapter on sitting for meditation, it was pointed out that the tip of the nose should provide only a momentary location for the gaze. A prolonged gaze on the nose or between the eyes with the inner gaze could strain the eye muscles. If any body part or process is to be taken as the focus of concentrative meditation, far and away the best choice is breathing – a technique of meditation to be described later in this chapter.

Ideally, any external object chosen for steady gaze meditation should be on a level with the eyes. An object placed a little below eye level will not tire the eyes, but one placed above eye level, so that the eyes have to turn up, will cause fatigue.

Sit firmly in one of the meditative postures, head, neck, and backbone in vertical line, motionless, breathing slowly and smoothly, looking steadily at the concentration-object. 'Cease from thine own activity, fix thine eye upon one point,' instructed Jacob Boehme, in one of his *Dialogues*. 'Gather in all thy thoughts and by faith press into the Centre.' Do not stare: look *through* the eyes rather than *from* them. The eyes should not be widely opened, as in a stare, or they will soon tire. Blink when necessary, or the eyes will become dry and painful. Frederick Spiegelberg, in *Spiritual Practices of India*, (58) says that the meditator should gaze 'in a calm, relaxed manner, somewhat as though he were looking at his face in a mirror.'

In early practice the attent on will slip away and unbidden thoughts will intrude and attempt to set up the chain reaction called reverie. Each time you become aware of having lost concentration, bring the torch beam of attention back to its task and produce again the soft impulse that sustains concentration for a while. You should look and feel serene. Poised in body and mind, simply *look*. When concentration is effortlessly sustained, subtler and deeper levels of mind will be known. And if you are concentrating upon, say, an apple or a rose, you will get to know it – its 'appleness' or 'roseness', what the Zen Buddhists call its 'suchness' – as you have never known it before.

AN EXPERIMENT IN VISUAL CONCENTRATION

In steady gaze meditation after a time the object concentrated upon becomes more vivid and luminous. Being held in the light of attention without interference from concepts and associations that normally operate in perception of this object, and without reflection, the perception strikes with a clarity and freshness such as one is likely to find in young children. Children do not have this freshness of vision for long: soon a mesh of categories acts upon every perception of known objcets. As the result of a study of eidetic imagery in children, H. Werner states (66):

> The image . . . gradually changes in functional character. It becomes essentially subject to the exigencies of abstract thought. Once the image changes in function and becomes an instrument in reflective thought, its structure will also change. It is only through such structural change that the image can serve as an instrument of expression in abstract mental activity. This is why, of necessity, the sensuousness, fullness of detail, the colour and vivacity of the image must fade.

Arthur J. Deikman (12), who has written several interesting papers on the nature of human consciousness and the modes of consciousness observed in mystical experience, sees mystic phenomena as 'a consequence of a deautomatization of the psychological structures that organize, limit, select, and interpret perceptual stimuli'. He carried out experiments in which subjects gazed steadily upon a blue vase, meditating in the Patanjali manner, though nothing so exotic or mystical was mentioned to the subjects. They were told (11):

> The purpose of the sessions is to learn about concentration. Your aim is to concentrate on the blue vase. By concentration I do not mean analyzing the different parts of the vase, or thinking a series of thoughts about the vase, or associating ideas to the vase; but rather, trying to see the vase as it exists in itself, without any connections to other things. Exclude all other thoughts or feelings or sounds or body sensations. Do not let them distract you, but keep them out so that you can concentrate all your attention, all your awareness on the vase itself. Let the perception of the vase fill your entire mind.

The instructions were, as we have seen, to use the blue vase as an object of Yogic concentration, though the subjects were not aware of this.

Each session of concentration lasted half an hour, and there were forty or more sessions spread over several months. The subjects' perceptions of the vase changed in directions similar to those reported by meditating Yogins – the vase became 'luminous', 'more vivid', 'I really began to feel, you know, almost as though the blue and I were perhaps merging or that the vase and I were. It was as though everything were sort of merging.'

Mr Deikman sees these changes as being a ' "deautomatization", an undoing of the usual ways of perceiving and thinking due to the special way that attention was being used.' He also sees these changes in consciousness as the working of a receptive mode, which research indicates is related to the right hemisphere of the brain; the contrasting acting mode (which predominates in the West) is related to the left hemisphere of the brain.

This experiment did not, of course, prove or disprove any of the metaphysical claims of the great religions, but it did give support to the changes in consciousness described by Patanjali and Raja Yogins.

A STABLE IMAGE EXPERIMENT

In another experiment which could throw light on steady gaze meditation, a group of physiological psychologists devised a method of keeping a visual image stable on the retina by use of a tiny projector mounted on a contact lens which the subject wears. The image from the projector falls constantly on the retina. Now normally our eyes keep on the move. The larger movements are called saccades, but there are tiny movements even when we try to hold the gaze motionless on some object. These tiny movements are called optical nystagmus.

The interesting thing about these experiments is that when the subjects looked at a stabilized image the image vanished. There was no visual experience whatever. A similar effect occurs when a subject gazes upon a completely clear visual field, a *ganzfeld*, such as a white-washed surface or the two halves of a table-tennis ball placed over the eyes. After about twenty minutes some subjects report a 'blank-out', a total disappearance of the sense of vision for a short period. Such a period is marked by a burst of alpha activity in the brain as recorded by an electroencephalogram (EEG). Similar alpha rhythms were recorded in the stabilized image experiment using a projector.

High alpha activity has been recorded in meditating Yogins and Zen monks.

Professor Robert E. Ornstein, in his book *The Psychology of Consciousness* (47), has pointed out the similarity of the 'blank out' experience to that of mystics who have taken meditation as far as the experience of 'void', 'white light', 'cloud of unknowing', and so on. He thinks the two experiences have 'essential similarities and are produced through quite similar procedures.' He also says:

> One consequence of the way our central nervous system is structured seems to be that, if awareness is restricted to one unchanging source of stimulation, a 'turning off' of consciousness of the external world follows. The common instructions for concentrative meditation all underscore this; one is advised to be constantly aware of the object of meditation and nothing else, to continuously recycle the same input over and over.

VISUALIZATION MEDITATION

> The Raja Yoga – By this knowledge the modifications of the mind are suspended, however active they may be: therefore, let the Yogi untiringly and unselfishly try to obtain this knowledge. When the modifications of the thinking principle are suspended, then one certainly becomes a Yogi: then is known the Indivisible, pure Gnosis.
>
> Let him contemplate on his own reflection in the sky as beyond the Cosmic Egg. . . . Through that let him think on the Great Void unceasingly. The Great Void, whose beginning is void, whose middle is void, whose end is void, has the brilliancy of tens of millions of suns, and the coolness of tens of millions of moons. By contemplating continually on this, one obtains success.

The above description of Contemplation of the Great Void, taken from the *Siva Samhita* (62), is one of the plainer examples of visualization meditation, which in Tantric and Tibetan Yoga can become elaborate and colourful fantasies. But however intricate the visualization, in the end the mind becomes still and clear and knows the white light of pure consciousness (*Purusha* or *Atman*).

A mental image of a flower, a tree, or a deity may be held in mind for a time, and then gradually dismantled, piece by piece, until only a clear light remains. Here is an example of this method, as described in *The Tibetan Book of the Dead* (19):

Whosoever thy tutelary deity may be, meditate upon the form for much time – as being apparent, yet non-existent in reality, like a form produced by a magician. . . . Then let the vision of the tutelary deity melt away from the extemities, until nothing at all remaineth visible of it; and put thyself in the state of the Clearness and the Voidness – which thou canst not conceive as something – and abide in that state for a little while. Again meditate upon the tutelary deity; again meditate upon the Clear Light; do this alternately. Afterwards allow thine own intellect to melt away gradually, beginning from the extremities.

Most of the visualization contemplations are much more complex than the two examples already given. However, there is a movement from complexity to clearness and voidness as contemplation moves from gross to luminous and subtle stages.

GROSS, LUMIMINOUS, AND SUBTLE CONTEMPLATION

A revered *guru*, god, or goddess is conjured up in gross contemplation (*sthula dhyana*). The appearance of the figure and the setting can be detailed and colourful. The *Gheranda Samitha* (61) gives two examples:

[Having closed the eyes] let him contemplate that there is a sea of nectar in the region of his heart: that in the midst of that sea an island of precious stones, the very sand of which is pulverized diamonds and rubies. That on all sides of it, Kadamba trees, laden with sweet flowers; that, next to those trees, like a rampart, a row of flowering trees, such as malati, mallika, jati, kesara, campaka, parijata and padma, and that the fragrance of these flowers is spread all round, in every quarter. In the middle of this garden, let the Yogin imagine that there stands a beautiful Kalpa tree, having four branches, representing the four *Vedas*, and that it is full of flowers and fruits. Beetles are humming there and cuckoos singing. Beneath that tree let him imagine a rich platform of precious gems, and on that a costly throne inlaid with jewels, and that on that throne sits his particular Deity as taught to him by his *Guru*. Let him contemplate on the appropriate form, ornaments and vehicle of that Deity. The constant contemplation of such a form is *Sthula Dhyana*.

Another Process: Let the Yogin imagine that in the pericarp of the great thousand-petalled Lotus [Brain] there is a smaller lotus having

> twelve petals. Its colour is white, highly luminous, having twelve bija letters, named ha, sa, ksa, ma, la, va, ra, ym, ha, sa, kha, phrem. In the pericarp of this smaller lotus there are three lines forming a triangle, a, ka, tha; having three angles called ha, la, ksa: and in the middle of this triangle, there is the *Pranava Om*. Then let him contemplate that there are two swans, and a pair of wooden sandals. There let him contemplate his *Guru Deva*, having two arms and three eyes, and dressed in pure white, anointed with white sandal-paste, wearing garlands of white flowers; to the left of whom stands *Sakti* of blood-red colour. By thus contemplating the *Guru*, the *Sthula Dhyana* is attained.

In contrast, luminous contemplation (*jyotir* or *tao dhyana*) is inner gazing upon the formless *Brahman*, the all-pervading cosmic spirit, manifesting itself as a mass of clear light. *Brahman* is contemplated again, as invisible cosmic energy, in subtle contemplation (*suksma dhyana*).

Though such heightened and developed powers of visualization in the service of contemplation may fascinate us, they cannot be said to belong to our practical approach to Yoga meditation, capable of quickly producing results on all the levels of approach described in the chapter entitled 'Why Meditate?' But, the techniques of meditation described in the rest of this chapter are accessible to all readers.

THOUGHT OBSERVATION AND REDUCTION

Vivekananda wrote (64):

> From our childhood upwards we have been taught only to pay attention to things external, but never to things internal, hence most of us have nearly lost the faculty of observing the internal mechanism. To turn the mind, as it were, inside, stop it from going outside, and then to concentrate all its powers, and throw them upon the mind itself, in order that it may know its own nature, analyse itself – is very hard work. Yet that is the only way to anything which will be a scientific approach to the subject.

To sit motionless, eyes closed, and look within the mind is not the simple matter that it first appears. The necessary awareness takes practice, and the difficulty lies not so much in doing as in having to be a mere passive spectator who must not interfere. It comes as a shock for the beginner to find what an unruly place his mind is: nevertheless, in this exercise, the role expected is that of a detached observer. In time the mind will become calmer and the number of thoughts active in it become less.

The method was described by Charles Baudouin in his book *Suggestion and Auto-suggestion* (4):

> Seat yourself for a while and allow your thoughts to take their own course freely. It [the mind] behaves like a frisky monkey. Let the monkey jump about; wait and take note. Your thoughts will entertain ugly ideas, so ugly that you will be surprised. But day by day, these errings will become less numerous and less extensive. During the first months you will have a thousand thoughts; then you will have no more than seven hundred; and the number will progressively diminish.

The image of an excitable monkey is one frequently used in Yogic literature in describing the mind. As you observe the parade of thoughts, note how they link by association – your personal associations based on conditioning, memory, and experience. It is essential to observe with detachment, to become a dispassionate spectator. Do not comment upon the thoughts; do not make judgments; do not show surprise, anger, dismay, sorrow, or any other emotion. Just observe the stream of thought with passive awareness.

After a time the number of thoughts will decrease. You will then be able to concentrate on single thoughts, to watch them rise, cross the mind, and go. Later on gaps will appear between thoughts, as though between beads on a thread. The space between the thoughts is more important than the thoughts themselves, which are unimportant in this exercise. The intervals between thoughts reveal pure awareness, the golden thread on which the beads of thought are strung. There, momentarily, one tastes the pure Self. That taste, however brief, is worth infinitely more than any number of words. 'He who tastes not, knows not,' said the Sufist Rumi.

BREATHING MEDITATION

Professor Ornstein, in *The Psychology of Consciousness* (47), tells how some American friends of his

> made a hopeful journey to India. Attracted by the repute of a certain famous *guru* (teacher) they hitchhiked across country, found a very inexpensive trans-Atlantic flight, and then travelled overland, with great difficulty, all the way to the Himalayas in the Indian subcontinent.

Finally, after walking for days and days, they reached the *ahram* (a sort of 'religious living association') of the *guru*. After allowing them some time to calm down, the *guru* saw them. Their hopes were high: perhaps they would receive a mysterious 'secret initiation' or maybe even a genuine 'magic word'. When they had outlined their trek, their difficulties, their expectations, and their hopes, the *guru* instructed them: 'Sit, facing the wall, and count your breaths. This is all.'

The technique of breathing meditation is well known in Yoga, Zen, and other schools of Buddhism, and has been mentioned many times in manuals on these disciplines. The seekers expected something more esoteric. In fact, the *guru's* 'This is all' was quite a lot. There is much that can be said for breathing meditation, especially for beginners, which most Westerners are.

Breathing meditation is accessible to all meditators and effective as a mental hygiene and for touching deep levels of energy and consciousness. Respiration provides an unchanging stimulus for Yogic concentrative meditation, is with us minute after minute throughout life, and accompanies us everywhere. Further: breath has close associations with the life-force (*prana*), and with subtle energy currents in the body, and consciousness itself. *Prana*, Yoga holds, is the connecting link between matter and mind. It is worth noting, also, that *Atman*, the Self to be realized, originally meant 'breath'. The German word *Atem* ('breath') has the same root as the Sanskrit *Atman*.

Some Yogins use the heartbeat as a focus for attention, but not all can acquire the knack of listening in to their heartbeats, nor do all find it the most suitable of concentration-objects, in spite of its being the pulse of life. The slower pace of breathing (slower than the beating heart) and its calming effect on the mind makes it an ideal process for contemplation. Within a few minutes of our seating ourselves motionless in poised posture, breathing slows down and becomes smoother. We can become conscious of our breathing instantly at any time and in any place, and fasten our attention on it quickly and easily. If we surrender to the respiratory rise and fall, inhalation and exhalation, we have the sensation not so much of breathing as of being breathed; and in an instant we are brought, in a way nothing else can do so effectively, close to our essential being.

Normally we only become aware of our breathing when we are agitated or excited, or have just made a strenuous physical effort;

but in breathing meditation we follow the slow smooth motions of calm breathing.

You can choose a point on which to fix the attention – either the point in the nose where incoming air first strikes or a point a little below the navel. This point in the belly is much favoured by Japanese Zen meditators, who stress its importance as the body's centre of gravity, and also the need for breathing deep into the belly. By fixing the attention there, thought is said to be 'nailed down'.

Breathe through the nostrils, unless they are so badly blocked that you are forced to breathe through you mouth. The meditative postures with head, neck and backbone in upright line favour deep healthful breathing. Readers who have already put into use the *pranayama* exercises given in *Yoga and Vitality* will have no problems here. As instructed there, breathe deeply into the adbomen; the diaphragm moves down and the ribs expand. The reverse process occur- during exhalation: the abdomen draws back and flattens, the diaphragm rises, and the thorax draws in. This deep diaphragmatic and abdominal breathing is beneficial to health, and the habit should be cultivated at *all* times. It relaxes and calms the mind, thus assisting meditation.

Once meditation commences the breathing should be left to itself without conscious regulation. Though one should breathe correctly, in the healthy, Yogic manner, during meditation, filling the lungs fully is not part of it. The motionless silence of sitting meditation requires only a small supply of oxygen. During meditation respiration will become slower, smoother, more rhythmic and, all meditation being a change from the gross to the subtle, finer. A text in Chinese Yoga says (38): 'The breath seems to have vanished in spite of the presence of the respiratory organs which seem to be useless; the practiser thus feels as if his breath comes in and out through the pores all over his body. This is the highest attainment in the art of breathing.'

Beginners should for a month or so count each breath they take, either on each inspiration or each expiration, from one to ten, and then go back to one. Counting beyond ten produces mounting mental effort and as the score increases the competitive element may intrude, which would mar the relaxed quality of meditation. Attention should be focused on one of the two places mentioned earlier: the point in the nostrils against which the incoming air is first felt to strike, or a place in the belly a little below the navel.

After a month of counting breaths, drop the counting. When the attention wanders to some distracting sound or sensation, or thoughts enter the mind, return once more to concentration on your breathing. Show no impatience. Return again and again. Eventually the number of interruptions of concentration will become much fewer – and one day, perhaps, there will be not meditator and his breathing, but a transcending of the subject-object dichotomy in the tranquillity of pure Being. It may only last a moment or so at first, but the experience is likely to be repeated subsequently in longer periods of peaceful union.

THE WITNESS

In this Yoga technique you observe any daily activity as though you were a detached and dispassionate spectator of yourself. This applies not only to your physical actions, but also to your states of mind. Detached, without passing judgments or commenting, be calmly aware of life's daily activities, whatever they may be: in the home, at work, in play, in social life, driving a car, emptying the bladder, eating a sandwich – there is no need to select activities, for whatever is being done *now* is the object of contemplative awareness. We learn a great deal about ourselves from self-observation, and the awareness leads to beneficial changes in the personality in the direction of greater equanimity, sensitivity, and alertness. We learn, too, the importance of the here and now, and to live more in the present.

The Buddhists call it 'mindfulness'. A Buddhist monk may be told to walk, and be mindful of every step. Walking becomes meditation. We have already seen that breathing can become meditation. Tibetan Yoga Masters instruct their pupils to make meditation exercises of their occupations: whether it be street cleaning, shoemaking, making pottery, clerking, serving in a shop, or whatever, every movement may be performed with contemplative awareness. Making a meditation exercise of everyday activities is common to many Buddhist schools. Asked 'What is Zen?', a Zen Master replied: 'When you are hungry eat, when you are tired sleep.' And Zen monks are said to receive sudden enlightenment (*satori*) on seeing a Master eat rice or perform some other everyday act.

Krishnamurti makes much of self-observation in his books and lectures, calling the mental attitude choiceless or passive awareness. Another name for it is bare attention. In the system of 'harmonious development' taught by George Gurdjieff it is known as self-remembering. Gurdjieff studied and worked with the Sufis and most of his exercises were of Sufic origin. Sufism uses the shell of Islam for its home, rather in the manner of the hermit crab, but claims to be the essence of all religions. Its methods have affinities with those of Yoga and other Eastern esoteric psychologies. It is customary in most of these systems to combine concentrative meditation in short sitting sessions once or twice a day with this more 'open' form of contemplation during everyday activity. Alternating contraction and expansion, one might say.

The Karma Yogin, who follows principally the path of service and action (*karma*), makes everyday activity a sacrament, an act of devotion to the divine principle. He fully attends to each action. The most commonplace activities of life are thus given a rich dimension through contemplative awareness.

VII Mantra Yoga

JAPA

Patanjali includes *japa* among a Yogin's observances. *Japa* is repetition of a letter, syllable, word, phrase, sentence, or sound considered to possess magical, occult, spiritual, or mystical potency, and called a *mantra*. It may be voiced aloud or thought inwardly. The latter technique has been made popular in the streamlined method taught by the *guru* Maharishi Mahesh Yogi under the name Transcendental Meditation. We will devote a separate chapter to TM, as it is known for short, and here discuss traditional methods.

Mantras are incantatory and mystical sounds. They provide a form of concentrative meditation. The voiced *mantra* should be repeated in a voice that is alive and resonant. The mystical aim is to utilize the power of sound vibrations to influence modalities of consciousness. A *mantra* may be repeated hundreds, even thousands of times.

As a Yoga method, *japa* has the virtue of simplicity, but can easily degenerate into arid, mechanical, and empty repetition. At its profoundest Mantra Yoga explores the influence of sound vibrations in a universe which science tells us is made up of vibrations. It is known that sound vibrations can destroy buildings and make people ill. That they can also have healing power is shown by the many successful experiments with music therapy.

LISTENING TO INTERNAL SOUNDS

Nada or listening to internal sounds is one of the practices of Mantra Yoga. The Yogin sits in a meditative posture and seals his right ear with his right thumb and his left ear with his left thumb, his eyes with his index fingers, his nostrils with his middle fingers, and his lips with the remaining four fingers.

The *Siva Samhita* (62) describes the variety of internal sounds that the Yogin should concentrate upon:

> From practising this gradually, the Yogi begins to hear the mystic sounds [*nadas*]. The first sound is like the hum of the honey-intoxicated bee, next that of a flute, then of a harp; after this, by the gradual practice of Yoga, the destroyer of the darkness of the world, he hears the sounds of ringing bells; then sounds like roar of thunder. When one fixes his full attention on this sound, being free from fear, he gets absorption [*Samadhi*].

MUSIC

The Mant Yogin is said to hear the sound of the cosmos, the music of the spheres, and in advanced meditation a single universal tone. The poet Schlegel wrote: 'Through all the tones there sounds, throughout the colourful earth, a gentle tone, sustained, for him who listens secretly.' Schumann used these lines to preface his *Fantasia* in C Major.

It is widely acknowledged that great music can communicate states of consciousness from composer to listener, in a language beyond words and so close to Being. When composing one of his symphonies, Gustav Mahler felt not so much that all his deepest questions had been answered as that there were no longer any questions to be asked. Hazrat Inayet Khan, a Sufi, says: 'Music is behind life and rules life: from music springs all life. The whole of creation exists in rhythm.'

POETRY

The incantatory element in Mantra Yoga is important. It should be recalled that it has made a considerable contribution to English and European poetry. Poetry differs from prose in having something of the quality of music, an incantatory element, and the words in good poetry say more than they mean in the narrower sense. In most national literatures, verse has preceded prose and has accompanied song and dance. Geoffrey Ashe, in a chapter on poetry in *The Art of Writing Made Simple* (1), says:

> Why this prevalence of rhythm? To answer the question is to identify the first word which we can supply to poetic language in general. It is *incantatory*. If that term conveys a hint of primitive magic, I cannot help it. The hint is justified. In fact the great themes of ancient poetry, the myths, may well have arisen out of earlier magic rituals. But however that may be, the incantatory quality is present in all true poems.

Poetry is the nearest language comes to expressing mystical experience. In England, for several centuries, the mystical tradition has been sustained more by poetry than by the Church. The philosopher Martin Heidegger suggests that poetry can lead us to Being. If so, it is a kind of Yoga.

OM (*AUM*)

Mantra Yoga belongs to the long history of man's striving to find the word whose utterance unlocks the door to Absolute Knowledge. Franz Kafka (31) summed up the search in a diary entry dated 18 October 1921:

> It is entirely conceivable that life's splendour forever lies in wait about each one of us in all its fullness, but veiled from view, deep down, invisible, far off. It *is* there, though not hostile, not reluctant, not deaf. If you summon it by the right word, by its right name it will come. This is the essence of magic, which does not create, but summons.

In Mantra Yoga magical or mystical potency has been ascribed to certain words, the most powerful of which is held to be OM. 'In the beginning was the Word.' To the Hindu that word is OM. It is the *pranava*, the 'word of glory', representing the Absolute.

This most famous of *mantras* is composed of three letters, AUM, which becomes OM on being voiced. The AU sound is pronounced as in the English 'house'. The AU sound begins at the back of the throat and comes forward to the front of the face, which singers call 'the mask'. The lips are closed for the M sound, which is usually sustained half as long again as the preceding AU sound.

The three letters AUM represent the aspects of *Brahman* or the Absolute found in the Hindu Trinity: Creator, Destroyer, and Preserver.

André van Lysebeth, a leading European teacher of Hatha Yoga, says (39) that the sounding of OM and other *mantric* vocables gives a vibro-massage to various glands and vital organs in the thoracic cavavity and the abdomen, stimulates deeper breathing, and tones the nervous system. But it is the influence on consciousness that concerns us in the Yoga of Meditation. The *Mundaka Upanishad* says: 'OM is the bow, the individual self is the arrow, the spirit is the target. One should then become one with it like the arrow that has penetrated the target.'

SOME OTHER MANTRAS

The *mantras* of Indian Yoga are usually Sanskrit letters, syllables, words, or sentences. *Mantras* other than OM are often preceded by it. The well-known OM MANI PADME HUM means 'OM, the jewel in the lotus.' In OM TAT SAT, TAT or 'That' refers to *Brahman*, and SAT is pure being. Two other well-known *mantras* are SOHAM, meaning 'He is I', and HANSAH, meaning 'I am He'.

As we shall see in the chapter on Bhakti Yoga, the Krishna Consciousness Movement have as the lynch-pin of their practice the *mahamantra* (great *mantra*): HARE KRISHNA, HARE KRISHNA, KRISHNA KRISHNA, HARE HARE, HARE RAMA, HARE RAMA, RAMA RAMA, HARE HARE. This is chanted again and again (*japa*).

KINDS OF *JAPA*

Japa can be performed in a variety of ways. If we look at Tantric practice we find the following kinds and methods:

i. Daily (*nitya*). Morning and evening as instructed by a *guru*.
ii Circumstantial (*naimittika*). For festival days and special occasions.
iii For desired results (*kamya*). With special attainments in mind.
iv Forbidden (*nishiddha*). Forbidden are the mixing of *mantras*, those from an unqualified instructor, those voiced incorrectly or without knowledge of their meaning.
v Penance (*prayaschitta japa*).
vi. Unmoving (*achala*). Immobile, firmly seated.
vii Moving (*chala*). While standing, sitting, lying, walking

about, or performing any activity. Repetition is inward; the lips do not move.

viii Voiced (*vachika*). Repeated aloud.

ix Whispered (*upanshu*). Only the practitioner hears the *mantra*.

x Bee (*bhramara*). The sound 'Ah' is produced low in the throat and sustained as long as is comfortable to a breath. A rapid inhalation is then made and the bee-sound repeated, and so on. It is sometimes called 'beetle-droning'.

xi Mental (*manasa*). Alain Danielou (9) calls this 'the very soul of *japa*. The *mantra* is not uttered aloud at all, but remains revolving in the mind. The eyes are closed. Meditation on the meaning of the *mantra* predominates over all other thoughts.'

xii Uninterrupted (*akhanda*). For those who have renounced the world. Continued for hours.

xiii Non-uttered (*a-japa*). The meaning of the *mantra* is held in the mind and absorbed.

xiv Circumambulatory (*pradakshina*). While walking in a temple or a garden.

MANTRAS IN OTHER TRADITIONS

The *mantra* method is not exclusive to Yoga. Concentrating and stilling the mind by repetition of words or sounds is found in other mystical traditions.

The priests of ancient Egypt saw the utterance of certain words in ritualistic moments as a way to open up consciousness to cosmic energies. The name of God or divinity is widely used for *japa* in other traditions. The Sufists perform *dhikr*, which means both 'repetition' and 'remembrance'. There is a tradition in the Pure Land Buddhism sect of Japan that if you can recite the *nembutsu* or name of Buddha once in the correct meaningful way, with the whole of your being, that is enough to produce enlightenment. Chanting *mantras* is the main method of another Japanese Buddhist sect, the Shingon-shu (Shingon means *mantra*). That the early Christians utilized a form of *japa* for concentrative meditation is clear from the contents of the *Philokalia*, a collection of writings by the Christian Fathers (first millenium), first published in Venice in 1782. The

'Prayer of the Heart' has remained a part of the Greek Orthodox tradition: 'Lord Jesus Christ, son of God have mercy upon me.' St John Climacus wrote: 'If many words are used in prayer, all sorts of distracting pictures hover in the mind but worship is lost. If little is said or only a single word pronounced, the mind remains concentrated.'

Transcendental Meditation, the method of deep relaxation and going to the source of thought taught by Maharishi Mahesh Yogi, is a streamlined presentation of one of the varieties of Mantra Yoga, silent repetition of a word. The Maharishi has made it the most wisely practised Yoga meditation in the West.

VIII The Transcendental Meditation of Maharishi Mahesh Yogi

MAHARISHI MAHESH YOGI

Maharishi Mahesh Yogi, the most widely known present-day *guru*, was born on 18 October 1911 in Uttar Kashi, son of an income tax official. He took a degree in physics at Allahabad University, worked for a time in a factory, and then in the early 1940s became a pupil of Swamī Brahmananda Saraswati, with whom he stayed thirteen years. After his teacher's death he went into seclusion for two years, during which he developed his method of Transcendental Meditation, a streamlined form of Mantra Yoga suited to the needs of active people. In 1959 he took the method to America and Europe. The publicity attendant on temporary associations with stars of the entertainments industry made the tiny, chuckling *guru* a household name in the western world. TM as it is known for short, has steadily gained adherents in many countries. Persons who enrol at a TM centre are not asked to alter their way of life, though it is believed that the influence of meditation will produce changes. Persons of all religions or none are welcomed, TM being a technique and not a religion or a philosophy. As a Hindu, Maharishi Mahesh Yogi believes in the law of *karma*, reincarnation, and other concepts given little support in the Western world; but non-Hindu meditators are not asked to renounce their own religious viewpoints, nor, for that matter, their worldly pleasures.

THE METHOD

The technique of Transcendental Meditation could hardly be simpler.

One mentally repeats a word while sitting still. The lips and tongue should not move. A Yoga sitting posture is not expected if the meditator does not find it comfortable. The eyes are closed and the attention is turned inwards. No mental force should be used: each time the mind is found to have wandered, the *mantra* is reintroduced.

At his or her initiation, each person who enrols for TM is given a Sanskrit word as a personal *mantra*. It is claimed that there is a specific word to suit the nervous system of each applicant. This, and a certain amount of mumbo-jumbo at the initiation, savours of an occultism out of step with the customary straightforward and commonsense presentation of the method. No real evidence has been offered in support of the claim, and some scepticism on this is expressed even within the organization. My view is that the choice of word is not of great importance either in Mantra Yoga or in TM – its *use* is what counts, leading the meditator to deep relaxation. It is necessary only that the word should be easily pronounced (Westerners report difficulty in this respect with some of the words given for TM) and that it should have no unpleasant or tension-producing associations. A meaningless word, which the Maharishi prefers, avoids distracting the attention with associated thoughts.

The Maharishi also insists that the method, simple though it is, cannot be taught by book instruction, and that meditators need to check progress with his personally-trained instructors.

He stresses the importance (as we did earlier in this book) of not thinking about or expecting results – that way, he says, the attention is undivided and the meditator will not 'fall victim to auto-suggestion and only imagine that experience.'

EFFORTLESS MEDITATION?

The Maharishi denies that the mind is controlled in Transcendental Meditation, and says that the mind moves naturally towards a field of greater happiness, which he calls bliss consciousness. This statement has led some of his followers to say that TM is not Yoga and that no Yogic concentration is involved. The Maharish has certainly simplified and streamlined a technique of Yoga, and he has himself said many times that TM is his version of Yoga meditation. His teaching that ascetism, austerity, strong will-power, and iron discipline are not needed and that the natural movements of the mind can be harnessed is timely, and welcomed by the majority of people today. However, I think one should be cautious about saying that no control and no concentration are involved in it, and that it is not a form of concentrative Yogic meditation. The Maharishi has developed a particularly easeful method of meditation, but it seems to me to be clearly within the mainstream Yogic tradition.

The Maharishi's instruction to repeat a *mantra* mentally, and to go back to it when the attention is found to have wandered from it, is familiar in all forms of concentrative Yoga meditation. Occasionally the writers of Yoga texts may employ metaphors that seem to imply a degree of iron control of the mind, but what is actually required is not concentration in the common Western sense of the word, as we made clear earlier in describing the right attitude to Yoga meditation. *All* Yoga meditation should be comfortable. Whatever the method used, to become aware that the attention has wandered is usually enough to switch it automatically back to its position. For example, the method of breathing meditation described earlier in this book can be just as easeful and gentle as Transcendental Meditation. It can be combined with use of the silent *mantra*, which is mentally repeated either on each inhalation or on each exhalation.

There is, moreover, a whole class of meditation which Claudio Naranjo calls 'opening-up', in contrast to the other main class of 'concentrative', meditation. The opening-up methods include the Zen meditation of 'just sitting' (*shikan-taza*), favoured by the Soto school, in which there is no object, not even a silent *mantra*, for the mind to fix on. Yet even here a meditative poise of mind, which is surely a kind of attention or concentration, is required. Zen Master Yasutani Roshi describes it thus: (68) 'Now, in *shikan-taza* the mind must be unhurried yet at the same firmly planted or massively composed, like Mount Fuji, let us say. But it also must be alert, stretched, like a taut bowstring. So *shikan-taza* is a heightened state of *concentrated* awareness wherein one is neither tense nor hurried, and certainly never slack.' (The italics are mine.)

The Maharishi appeared to concede that concentration, of however natural a kind, was involved in TM in reply to a question I heard put to him at a press conference in London's Festival Hall in 1974. Asked whether the repetition of a *mantra* was not a form of concentration, the *guru* skilfully replied, with one of his famous chuckles, that in this TM was 'using a thorn to remove a thorn from the flesh'. Using a thorn nevertheless.

That there is more to this than just semantic confusion is clear from a few words (16) spoken by the Maharishi in a television discussion which was transmitted by the British Broadcasting Corporation on 5 July 1964: 'We, in meditation, don't make an effort. We allow the mind to get into these more effortless [*sic*] states, because in experiencing the subtlest state of thought, effort is less and less, and less, and less, and then no effort, absolutely no effort.'

So only the deeper stages of meditation are effortless. The dive may be effortless, but only after one has walked to the end of the springboard and made the jump in the correct manner. In TM the silent *mantra* provides the springboard. Similarly, Patanjali's *dharana* gives way to *dhyana*, which flows effortlessly into *samadhi* – what the Maharishi calls bliss consciousness.

TM LABORATORY-TESTED

Laboratory research into Transcendental Meditation reveals that during meditation the following physiological changes occur:

- i Heartbeat and breathing rates slow down.
- ii Oxygen consumption and metabolicnate falls by twenty per cent.
- iii The blood lactate level drops. This level goes up with stress and fatigue.
- iv Skin resistance to electric current increase fourfold, a sign of relaxation.
- v EEG readings of brain wave patterns shown increased alpha activity – again a sign of relaxation.

These findings, in subjects who had been meditating between one month and nine years, show that TM induces deep relaxation even though the meditator is neither asleep nor in a hypnotic trance.

For the claim that TM releases 'creative intelligence' there has not been any reliable evidence.

THE SOURCE OF THOUGHT

The Maharishi equates the mentally 'sounded' *mantra* with thought, which is 'the subtle state of speech' and 'a subtle form of sound'. He likens the rise of a thought to surface consciousness to a bubble that rises to the surface of the ocean. In his *Science of Being* (41) he says:

> A thought starts from the deepest level of consciousness and rises through the whole depth of the ocean of mind until it finally appears as a conscious thought at the surface. Thus we find that every thought stirs the whole range of the depth of consciousness but is consciously appreciated only when it reaches the conscious level; all its earlier stages of development are not appreciated.

By repeatedly diving down during meditation – compare this with the analogy of a pilot flying in and out of clouds used in discussing Raja Yoga – thought can be known at all the points of its journey to the surface of consciousness. At its subtlest level thought is transcended.

> When the conscious mind transcends the subtlest level of thought, it transcends the subtlest state of relative experience and arrives at the transcendental Being, the state of pure consciousness or self-awareness. This is how, in a systematic manner, the conscious mind is led, step by step, to the direct experience of transcendental absolute Being.

The Maharishi says that Being cannot be experienced through any of the senses, which are in the relative field. Sensory perception is transcended in 'a state of consciousness in which the experiencer no longer experiences'. This comes about for reasons we made clear in discussing Patanjali's Raja Yoga: knower, known, and knowing become one.

LEVELS OF CONSCIOUSNESS

One does not have to read the writings of Maharishi Mahesh Yogi long to discover that he is teaching, in his own way, the *upanishadic* creed of finding the Self and knowing it to be one with *Brahman*.

He says that by meditating one reaches a state of consciousness beyond the well-known states of dreamless sleep, dreaming sleep, and wakefulness. This fourth state he calls Transcendental Consciousness. Its physiological concomitant is deep relaxation. Beyond this stage are three more.

The fifth stage is Cosmic Consciousness, in which Transcendental Consciousness is carried into everyday activity. In Cosmic Consciousness, one acts, but is aware that the Self is untouched by action. The Maharishi says that Cosmic Consciousness can be achieved through meditation alone, and by the ordinary man without his becoming a recluse or undergoing harsh disciplines.

It is more difficult to reach the final two stages. In God Consciousness the Self and activity are united. The final stage is called Union. In it one 'looks out on the world with the eyes of God'.

DR HERBERT BENSON AND THE 'RELAXATION RESPONSE'

The manuscript of this book was already going to press when I read with great interest Dr Herbert Benson's *The Relaxation Response* (William Morrow, New York, 1976). Here was laboratory-tested confirmation of views I expressed earlier in this chapter.

In 1968 Dr Benson and colleagues at the Harvard Medical School studied the physiological changes during meditation of volunteer practitioners of Transcendental Meditation. The findings were those mentioned above – a marked decrease in the body's oxygen consumption (hypometabolism), the production of Alpha waves in the brain, and so on. Dr Benson's findings are much quoted by the 'sellers' of TM, as one might expect. But they do not mention Dr Benson's subsequent studies and findings, which he described in *The Relaxation Response*.

Dr Benson says that the physiological changes seen in meditators using the TM technique are duplicated by other techniques of meditation, as long as four basic factors are present: (1) A quiet environment; (2) A mental device that provides a constant stimulus; (3) A passive attitude that does not worry about distracting thoughts; (4) a comfortable position.

Dr Benson himself teaches the simple technique of combining silent repetition of a word with awareness of breathing – the combination suggested earlier in this chapter and which I have used effectively for several years. His patients sit comfortably, close their eyes, become aware of their breathing, and mentally repeat the word 'One' on each exhalation.

Dr Benson's own words should be quoted: 'It is important to remember that there is not a single method that is unique in eliciting the Relaxation Response. For example, Transcendental Meditation is one of the many techniques that incorporate these [four] components. However, we believe it is not necessary to use the specific method and specific *secret*, personal sound taught by Transcendental Meditation. *Tests at the Thorndike Memorial Laboratory of Harvard have shown that a similar technique used with any sound or phrase or prayer or mantra brings forth the same physiologic changes noted during Transcendental Meditation* . . . In other words using the basic necessary components, any one of the age-old or the newly derived techiques produces the same physiologic results regardless of the mental device used.' (*The Relaxation Response*, pp 113-4).

Dr Benson's investigations lead him to believe that 'the passive attitude is perhaps the most important element in eliciting the Relaxation Response'. This would explain the effectiveness of Transcendental Meditation – for Maharishi Mahesh Yogi attaches supreme importance to effortlessness – the passive attitude – in his simple, streamlined technique.

IX Yantra Yoga

FORM-SYMBOLS

At the same time that the sound symbol (*mantra*) is being repeated (*japa*), a form or design symbol (*yantra*) may be gazed upon. It may also be a single means of concentrative contemplation. *Yantras* represent in the visual field what *mantras* represent in the aural. They are diagrams drawn for the purpose of finding the centre of one's being or Self-realization. As art works to be gazed upon they range from the simple to the colourful and elaborate. *Yantra* meditation is practised mainly by the Yogins of Tantric Hinduism and Tantric Buddhism.

The Yogin sits in a meditative posture and concentrates on the form-symbol with his gaze, holding the mind steady and opening to the deep meaning of the symbol. Some forms of *yantra* meditation include a psychic journey before the mind becomes silent. Some Yogins close their eyes and visualize the *yantra*, holding it firmly in the mind.

MANDALAS

The most notable and elaborate *yantras* are the *mandalas* in which the designer includes concentric circles, sometimes within a square. *Mandala* is a Hindu word meaning 'circle', and a circle is the most important oriental symbol for unity and wholeness. It is the symbol of the Self. Its artistic representation is an object of contemplation whereby the state of consciousness it objectifies is evoked in the beholder.

Forms of the *mandala* in Christian symbolism are the nimbus and the rose window; the central symbol (*yantra*) of Christianity is the cross, however. In Zen painting the circle represents enlightenment and human perfection. Circles called 'sun wheels' appear in rock engravings that date back to the Neolithic age, before the invention of the wheel. *Mandala* construction (of a simple kind) and meditation is even found among the Eskimos. Peter Freuchen, in his *Book of the Eskimos* (20) tells how an Eskimo will sit before a large stone and with a small sharp stone start carving a circle upon the large stone. He will continue the circular movement for hours, sometimes days, until he passes into a trance.

Professor Eliade (17), an eminent authority on religious symbols, here describes the function of the *mandala* in both its external and its interiorized form:

> The term itself means 'a circle'; the translations from the Tibetan sometimes render it by 'centre' and sometimes by 'that which surrounds'. In fact a *mandala* represents a whole series of circles, concentric or otherwise, inscribed within a square; and in this diagram, drawn on the ground by means of coloured threads or coloured rice powder, the various divinities of the Tantric pantheon are arranged in order. The *mandala* thus represents an *imago mundi* and at the same time a symbolic pantheon. The initiation of the neophyte consists, among other things, in his entering into the different zones and gaining access to the different levels of the *mandala*. This rite of penetration may be regarded as equivalent to the well-known rite of walking round a temple (*pradakshina*), or of the progressive elevation, terrace by terrace, up to the 'pure lands' at the highest levels of the temple. On the other hand, the placing of the neophyte in a *mandala* may be likened to the initiation by entry into a labyrinth: certain *mandalas* have, moreover, a clearly labyrinthine character. The function of the *mandala* may be considered at least two fold, as is that of the labyrinth. On the one hand, penetration into a *mandala* drawn on the ground is equivalent to an initiation ritual; and, on the other hand, the *mandala* 'protects' the neophyte against every harmful force from without, and at the same time helps him to concentrate, to find his own 'centre'.
>
> But every Indian temple, seen from above, is a *mandala*. Any Indian temple is, like a *mandala*, a microcosm and at the same time a pantheon. Why, then, need one construct a *mandala* – why did they want a new 'Centre of the World'? Simply because, for certain devotees, who felt in need of a more authentic and a deeper religious experience, the traditional ritual had become fossilised: the construction of a fire altar or the ascent of the terraces of a temple no longer enabled them to redis-

cover their 'centre'. Unlike archaic man or the man of Vedic times, the Tantric devotee had need of a *personal experience* to reactivate certain primordial symbols in his consciousness. That is why, moreover, some Tantric schools rejected the external *mandala*, and had recourse to interiorised *mandalas*. These could be of two kinds: first, a purely mental construction, which acted as a 'support' for meditation, or, alternatively, an identification of the *mandala* in his own body. In the former case the yogi places himself mentally within the *mandala*, and thereby performs an act of concentration and, at the same time, of 'defence' against distraction and temptation. The *mandala* 'concentrates'; it preserves one from dispersion, from distraction. The discovery of the *mandala* in his own body indicates a desire to identify his 'mystical body' with a microcosm.

The *maṅdala* concentrates and integrates the mind of the meditator; he makes a psychic journey, entering the *mandala*, and passing to its centre so that the centre of his Being and that of the *mandala* coincide.

The psycho-analyst C. G. Jung made the discovery that some mentally-ill patients, when given a box or paints or crayons, will draw *mandala* shapes without being aware of their significance. He found *mandala* depiction most frequent in patients moving towards psychic wholeness, a process he termed Individuation. The circle motif also appeared in the dreams of such patients.

5 The Ganapati Yantra

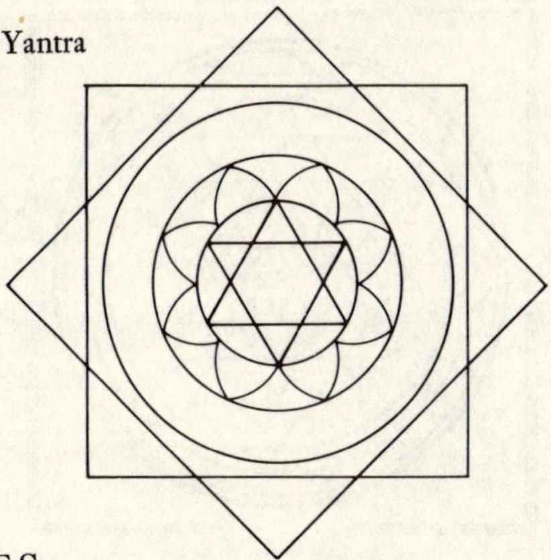

TRIANGLES

Triangles surrounded by concentric circles appear frequently in

Hindu *yantras*. The triangles usually interpenetrate, some pointing down and some pointing up. A triangle pointing up represents Siva, the male cosmic principle, and one pointing down represents Shakti, the female cosmic principle. A central point (*bindi*) represents *Brahman*, the Absolute. The word *bindu* has a number of meanings and shades of meaning. It is a dot or period, vitalizing a consonant when placed above it; it is seed; it is semen; it is Void or Emptiness.

Aniela Jaffe, in her contribution to the book *Man and his Symbols* (27), writes:

> But a great many of the eastern meditation figures are purely geometrical in design; these are called *yantras*. Aside from the circle, a very common *yantra* motif is formed by two interpenetrating triangles, one point-upward, the other point-downward. Traditionally, this shape symbolizes the union of Shiva and Shakti, the male and female divinities, a subject that also appears in sculpture in countless variations. In terms of psychological symbolism, it expresses the union of opposites – the union of the personal, temporal world of the ego with the non-personal, timeless world of the non-ego. Ultimately, this union is the fulfilment and goal of all religions: it is the union of the soul with God. The two interpenetrating triangles have a symbolic meaning similar to that of the more common circular *mandala*. They represent the wholeness of the psyche or Self, of which consciousness is just as much a part of the unconscious.

6 The Mandala of the Srichakra

The mandala of the *srichakra* has nine basic triangles that represent 'nine fundamental natures' or 'nine wombs' whereby 'duality evolves from unity', corresponding to the nine elements of which we are composed: skin, blood, flesh, fat and bones, known as the 'five damsels of Siva', plus the 'four *srikantha*' (*srikantha* is another name for Siva), which are marrow, seed, vital energy and individual soul (*jiva*).

The *srichakra* is another name for the *sahasnana chaktra*, 'the lotus of a thousand petals', the highest of the *chakras* or energy centres of the subtle body, located at the tip of the head. This *mandala* thus represents the successful ascent of latent force, called *kundalini* or serpent power, to the *srichakra*. This movement is achieved through intense concentrative meditation (*mantra* and *yantra*) and advanced breath controls. This branch of Yoga, hazardous unless under the personal direction of a reliable *guru*, is called Laya or Kundalini Yoga.

X Kundalini (Serpent Power) Yoga

Nothing that has been written in either the classic or the modern literature of Yoga gives us an opening to fit *kundalini* into our practical approach. All accounts agree that intensive and even hazardous discipline for many years is required by this Yoga path, which can be traced back to the Indus Valley civilization which ended about 3000 BC, and probably was known before that.

The method is a combination of concentrative meditation, which utlizes *mantras* and *yantras*, breath controls, and muscular contractions (*mudras*) and locks (*bandhas*). Some of the *mudras* and *bandhas* were described in *Yoga and Vitality*, but they were given there for the purpose of enhancing sexual health and fitness. Breathing exercises (*pranayama*), also described in *Yoga and Vitality* are considered an essential preliminary to attempting to arouse the body's latent power as they purify the channels (*nadis*) through the energy flows. As the methods of awakening *kundalini* are complex and not without danger, and require expert supervision, they will not be described here. However, we will concisely indicate the salient concepts of Kundalini Yoga, also called Laya (Latent Power) Yoga.

These are:

- i *Kundalini* or serpent power is an energy latent in the body, said to be coiled at the base of the spine.
- ii The *chakras* or vital centres represent stages in the ascent of the power.
- iii The *sushumna* is the channel which carries the *kundalini* force.
- iv Bliss consciousness (*samadhi*) is triggered when *kundalini* has travelled via the *sushumna* and through the vital centres to the highest *chakra*, the *sahasrara*, the 'thousand-petalled lotus' at the crown of the head.

SERPENT POWER

The concept of a key universal energy that can be activated in the body and controlled by meditation is found in a number of esoteric traditions. Life-energy theories have a long history in India, China, Japan, Korea, and Hawaii. In Yoga the universal force has aspects as Shakti, the female creative power, and as *prana*, which has also a meaning as 'breath'. The latent force within the body is called *kundalini*, or serpent power. Yogins always refer to *kundalini* as 'she'.

According to Yogic tradition, *kundalini* is a concentration of Cosmic Life Energy or *prana-Shakti*, dormant at the base of the spine and symbolically represented as a serpent, coiled three and a half times, closing with her mouth the entrance to the fine channel (*sushumna*) leading upwards through the spinal cord to the crown of the head, where Siva awaits, triggering *samadhi*. The ascending force passes through several key centres, called *chakras*, of which by main tradition there are seven.

WILHELM REICH

Kundalini force is referred to variously by writers as electro-magnetic energy, psychic force, and so on – but its nature remains a mystery.

Supporters of the orgone energy theory of the Austrian psycho-analyst and natural scientist Wilhelm Reich point out the similarities between Reich's concept of cosmic energy and the Yogic *prana*, and between his theory of bodily 'rings' and the *chakras*. Some neo-Reichians shy off the term 'orgone', but common to all Reichian therapists is his idea of a flow of energy in the body which if blocked causes illness.

For an account of Reich's theories on vital energies see W. Edward Mann's *Orgone, Reich and Eros*. There Professor Mann says (42): 'Indian thinking, both Hindu and yoga, on the body, its energy basis and potentials, is very similar to Reich's. Already some young Reichians are attempting to integrate the two approaches; given the interest of many Western youth in Oriental concepts and philosophy, we can expect interesting developments from such combinations.'

CHAKRAS

The *chakras*, literally 'wheels', are said to be vortices of *pranic* energy, each associated with special powers that can be awakened by concentrative meditation. However, there are three approaches to interpreting these vital centres. The first equates them with nerve plexuses, glands, or actual centres, in the body. Such equations are only partly successful. A second view is that the *chakras* belong to a subtle or astral body, the *sukshma sharira*. The third idea is that the *chakras* are symbols indicating points for concentrative meditation. The first and second approaches have been those most frequently promulgated. Indries Shah indicates that the Sufis take the third view in relation to *lataif*, which has similarities to the *chakra* system (56): 'In Yoga, the *chakras* or *padmas* are conceived as physically located centres in the body, linked by invisible nerves or channels. Yogis generally do not know that these centres are merely concentration points, convenient formulations whose activation is part of a theoretical working hypothesis.'

The most recent attempt to show *kundalini* as a biological phenomenon is by Gopi Krishna, whose Research Foundation for *Kundalini* has branches in Europe and North America.

The symbology of the *chakras* is complex and highly imaginative. In most cases a *chakra* has its seed sound-symbol (*bija-mantra*), its form symbol (*yantra*), its colour, its presiding god and goddess, and so on. The lower five *chakras* correspond to the five elements. The coiled serpent sleeps in the lowest *chakra* (*muladhara*).

Buddhist Tantrists recognize only four *chakras*, the first at the navel, and the fourth in the head. Some ancient statues depict the Buddha with a swelling on the top of the head indicating the activated brain *chakra* (*usnisa-kamala*).

The seven *chakras* of Kundalini Yoga, with their main symbols and associations, are as follows:

Root Centre (*Muladhara Chakra*)
Location: base of the spine, between the anus and the genitals. Form-symbol: lotus with four petals. Sound symbol: *lam*. Colour: yellow. Element: earth. Presiding god: Brahma the Creator. Goddess: Dakini.

Pelvic Centre (*Swadhistana Chakra*)
Location: at the genitals. Form-symbol: lotus with six petals. Sound symbol: *vam*. Colour: white. Element: water. Presiding god: Vishnu. Goddess: Rakini.

Solar Plexus Centre (*Manipura Chakra*)
Location: at the solar plexus. Form-symbol: lotus with ten petals. Sound symbol: *ram*. Colour: red. Element: fire. Presiding god: Rudra. Goddess: Lakini.

Heart Centre (*Anahata Chakra*)
Location: at the heart. Form-symbol: lotus with twelve petals. Sound-symbol: *yam*. Colour: blue. Element: air. Presiding god: Isha. Goddess: Kakini.

Throat Centre (*Vishuddha Chakra*)
Location: at the throat. Form-symbol: lotus with sixteen petals. Sound-symbol: *ham*. Colour: white. Element: ether. Presiding god: Sadashiva. Goddess: Sakini.

Brow Centre (*Ajna Chakra*)
Location: between the eyebrows, the 'third eye'. Form-symbol: lotus with two petals. Sound-symbols: OM (AUM). Colour: snow white. Presiding goddess: Hakini.

Crown of the Head Centre (*Sahasrara Chakra*)
Location: at the cerebrum. Form-symbol: lotus with a thousand petals. Presiding god: Siva. This is the centre of Self-realization (*samadhi*).

The rich and colourful symbolism of the *chakras* goes far beyond the concise summary given above.

THE *SUSHUMNA*

The *sushumna* is the fine channel which carries *kundalini* energy. Taking the two main views, it is either physically located as the vagus or pneumogastric, the tenth cranial nerve, or is considered to be part of the invisible network of channels of the astral body. The former view is argued in detail by Dr Vansant Rele in *The Mysteri-*

ous Kundalini (53); he also states the case for the *chakras* being nerve plexuses. On either side of the astral tube or *sushumna* run two other tubes called *ida* and *pingala*, which carry nerve currents up and down the body.

SELF-REALIZATION

Throughout its long history Kundalini Yoga has been practised by persons seeking magical and occult powers. The writers of Tantric texts in their enthusiasms have exaggerated such powers, and also are guilty of oversimplyfing the means to success. A single *mantra* or *mudra* is credited with the power to raise *kundalini* to 'the thousand-petalled lotus' in the cerebrum. The result is *samadhi*, the realization of the true Self beyond the ego that is the goal of all the Yogas.

The process of raising *kundalini* from *chakra* to *chakra* can take hours of psycho-physical control and concentrative meditation, and it may take decades of regular practice before the brow centre is reached, if it ever is. According to the jacket blurb of the British edition of his *Secret of Yoga* (35), Gopi Krishna, after seventeen years of meditation, 'unexpectedly experienced the awakening of *kundalini*, and subsequent severe ordeals which few have survived.' And Swami Vishnudevananda (63) says that only a few famous Yogins have taken serpent power to the crown of the head. As things now stand, *kundalini* is not the easiest of paths to the Self.

XI Yoga of Action (Karma)

WISDOM IN ACTION

Karma Yoga is called 'the Yoga of Action' (*karma* means 'action'), but it must be understood that a special quality of action is intended, one far removed from the 'go-getting' so admired in the Western world. This special quality at its purest is called actionless action (*naishkarmya karma*), and results from non-attachment (*vairagya*). In the *Bhagavad Gita*, in which the most inspired instruction in 'the way of action' is to be found, the need for non-attachment is stressed again and again, but this is only really complete when the individual has found and lives in his Self (*Purusha* or *Atman*), which is untouched by action and is over and above it as pure Being.

By the universal law of *karma*, good actions beget good results and likewise evil action produce evil results. Intentions count as actions, and one does not suffer for unintentional evil actions. Thoughts, good or bad, normally tend to be acted out in some way, and may become habits. Hence the saying: 'We sow a thought, we reap an act. We sow an act and reap a habit. We sow a habit and reap a judgment.' The law of *karma* is at work in our dealings with wife, children, parents, relations, colleagues in work, and so on. The Hindu believes he has future lives – a great many of them if need be – to build up *karmic* credit to effect release from the round of rebirths. Few people in the Western world believe in reincarnation, but we can all see how to some extent our thoughts, actions, and habits build up a store of future misfortune or future good for us in this one life we are sure of.

Despite a relationship with the law of *karma*, Karma Yoga does not make much of good and bad deeds, in the sense of listing them and reiterating warnings against 'sin' or 'wickedness'. The emphasis is on non-attachment, and action performed with full attention in the here and now and in a spirit of care and compassion – love guided by wisdom.

Karma Yoga is wisdom in work and action. The Karma Yogin's actions are marked by poise of body, mind, and spirit. In this the other main Yogas can make their contribution: Hatha Yoga for better posture, balance, and relaxation; Raja Yoga for equanimity and control of mind: Jnana Yoga for knowledge of Self; and Bhakti Yoga to impart a feeling tone of love and worship to all life's activities, even the humblest. Karma Yogins reinforce wisdom in work and action with set periods of meditation for mental hygiene and deeper insight, but there is a sense in which meditation and contemplation are possible at any moment. Each action, when performed with right attention, becomes contemplative. A similar approach is found in Buddhism: Zen Buddhists talk of 'every moment Zen (Zen means 'meditation'). A Zen Master, asked 'What is Zen? replied: 'When you are hungry eat, when you are tired sleep.'

In Karma Yoga, love and duty having become one, duties become sources of happiness. The dustman who performs his work with mindfulness is the equal of the surgeon performing a delicate operation in the same spirit, and superior in Yogic terms if the latter works only with thought of the money he will receive. Right attitude is all-important.

Karma Yoga is seen at its finest in a life of service. Mahatma Gandhi exemplified the spirit of Karma Yoga; Albert Schweitzer could also be mentioned in this connection.

Karma Yoga means service and work without clinging to the frui s of action. This is a difficult concept for Westerners to grasp. More often than not it leads to a rich return in efficiency, effectiveness, and productivity. A poised detachment from work, accompanied by steady application, is a sure technique for consistent and skilled results.

GITA YOGAS

Karma Yogins turn to the *Bhagavad Gita* for inspirational instruction in the Way of Action. This great work, which calls itself a Yoga scripture, is not without appeal for Westerners: over a hundred translations have been made into English and other European languages. The chapter headings reveal that the *Gita's* range of instruction is not so much Yoga as Yogas – Samkhya Yoga, Karma Yoga, Jnana Yoga, Sannyasa Yoga, Dhyana Yoga, Vijnana Yoga, Abhyasa Yoga, Bhakti Yoga. There is also mention in the text of Buddhi Yoga and Atman Yoga. The nature of these Yogas can be summarized as follows:

Samkhya Yoga – Yoga of Science (literally 'number')
Karma Yoga – Yoga of Action
Jnana Yoga – Yoga of Self-knowledge
Sannyasa Yoga – Yoga of Renunciation
Dhyana Yoga – Yoga of Meditation
Vijnana Yoga – Yoga of Comprehension
Abhyasa Yoga – Yoga of Steady Effort
Bhakti Yoga – Yoga of Devotion
Buddhi Yoga – Yoga of Wisdom
Atman Yoga – Yoga of Self

There is considerable overlapping of the Yogas, so that it is virtually impossible to practice any one of the above Yogas without practising several of the others. Things become less confused if we reduce the Yogas to three that between them absorb all the others. These are Karma Yoga, Jnana Yoga, and Bhakti Yoga.

Lord Krishna's instruction to Arjuna in the discourses of the *Gita* overlaps with that given by Patanjali in his *Yoga Sutras*. In both works one finds the key sequence of internal Yoga – concentration (*dharana*), contemplation (*dhyana*), and Self-realization (*samadhi*). The insights gained by meditation are to be carried into everyday action. The Yogin established in wisdom goes about his duties with actionless action, a paradoxical and difficult concept also taught in Taoism and Zen, in which it is called non-action (*wu-wei*).

NON-ATTACHMENT

Non-attachment (*vairagya*) is the key to practising Karma Yoga. It is often misinterpreted by Westerners as apathy, indifference, or coldness: it is true that the writers of the old Yoga texts, by their use of forceful simile and metaphor, often give that impression.

In the second discourse of the *Gita*, Lord Krishna instructs:

2, 47. Thy concern is with action alone, never with results. Let not the fruit of action be thy motive, nor let thy attachment be for inaction.
2, 48. Steadfast in devotion do thy works, O Dhanamjaya, casting off

attachment, being the same in success and failure. Evenness is called Yoga. . . .

2, 51. For men of wisdom cast off the fruit of action; possessed of knowledge [and] released from the bond of birth, they go to the place where there is no evil.

Krishna and Arjuna hold their conversation on a battlefield, shortly before the start of the battle. Arjuna is told by the god that he is committed to action in the relative world; he cannot do otherwise. However, the young warrior must act while aware of the Self within that is untouched by action. And he must act without thought of result. Which is not the same thing as not having any aims, not caring, or not accepting the result when it comes.

Maharishi Mahesh Yogi (40) comments on Discourse 2, verse 47:

This does not mean that Arjuna is not to fight for the sake of winning the battle; it does not mean that the action should be done without caring for its result. That would be hypocrisy.

It is the anticipated fruit of an action that induces a man to act. It is desire for a result that makes him begin to act and enables him to persist in the process of action. The Lord wishes to show that the result of the action will be greater if the doer puts all his attention and energy into the action itself, if he does not allow his attention and energy to be distracted by thinking of results. The result will be according to the action, there is no doubt about that. . . .

The teaching of non-anticipation of the fruit of action has an even deeper, cosmic significance in that it is supported by the very process of evolution. If a man is held by the fruit of action, then his sole concern is centred on the horizontal plane of life. Seeing nothing higher than the action and its fruit, he loses sight of the Divine, which pervades the action and is the almighty power at its basis leading it to ultimate fulfilment. He thus loses contact with the vertical plane of life, on which the process of evolution is based.

Thus it is clear that the lord's teaching on the one hand supports activity and on the other upholds evolution and freedom.

Non-attachment means not clinging to objects, emotions, images, ideas. One cannot avoid action, one cannot avoid things; but it is possible to act without having an attitude of posessiveness. The Sanskrit word *niryogakshema* is used in the *Gita* to convey the state of being 'independent of possessions' – which does not mean not having any at all (though Yogins generally make do with very little) but carries the meaning that (41) 'in this state one is not required to think of gaining what one does not have or of preserving what one has.'

We are speaking now of a kind of streamlined living that finds delight in the most important things, which are also seen to be the simplest things. In this way one acts free from bondage to things. So many people are held captive by their possessions, though they think it is the other way round.

In Discourse 3 Lord Krishna teaches Arjuna that every action should be performed as an act of devotion, as a sacrifice (*yajna*). With clear vision, obtained by Yoga, it will be obvious where one's duty lies and one acts accordingly. The man with knowledge of the Self (*Atman* or *Purusha*) is capable of actionless action (*naishkarmya karma*). He acts because one cannot live in the relative world without acting, but he is not the slave of things – whether material objects, emotions, or thought. Having an attitude of non-grasping and non-anticipating, he is free to give his total attention to what he is doing in the manner which the Buddhists call mindfulness, which is the total man totally attending. Thus pruning a rose bush, buttoning a coat, typing a manuscript, boiling an egg, ironing a shirt, and any of the multiplicity of crafts, arts, trades, and professions becomes a form of contemplation and at the same time a form of worship.

'The place where there is no evil,' referred to in the *Gita* 2, 51, is the state of spiritual freedom (*Moksha*). The highest non-attachment is found in the liberated Yogin.

THE *GITA'S* TEACHING OF KARMA YOGA

The key passages in the *Bhagavad Gita* giving guidance on Karma Yoga occur in the third discourse. The following verses were translated into English by A. Mahadeva Sastri. The commentary given within quotation marks is that by the philosopher Sankaracharya, whose name is spelt in several other ways – *acharya* means 'religious teacher'. He is thought to have lived between 510 and 478 BC, though some scholars place him later.

3, 3. In this world a two fold path was taught by Me at first, O sinless one: that of the *Samkyhas* by devotion to knowledge, and that of the Yogins by devotion to action.

The understanding gained by Jnana Yoga, the Yoga of Knowledge, and by contacting pure consciousness by meditation, can be carried into everyday action and action iteself can be a form of contemplation in the way described earlier. It is understandable that the path of Karma Yoga should be deemed suitable for people caught up in family, social, and commercial life. Karma is the Yoga of the market place, but the Self-realized Yogin is untouched by its clamour and its profusion of sense stimuli and objects of consciousness.

3, 4. Not by abstaining from action does man win actionlessness, nor by mere renunciation does he attain perfection.

'By abstaining from action man cannot attain to actionlessness (*naishkarmya*), freedom from activity, i.e. devotion in the path of knowledge, the condition of the actionless Self.' *Naishkaryma* can also be translated as 'non-action' or 'actionless action'. One acts, but in the knowledge that the Self is not touched.

3, 5. None, verily, even for an instant, ever remains doing no action; for every one is driven helpless to action by the energies born of nature.

'The energies (*gunas*) are three, *Sattva*, *Rajas* and *Tamas*. "Every one" means every living being that is ignorant [*ajna*], who knows not [the Self]; for, it is said of a wise man that he is one "who is unshaken by the energies" (14, 23).' 14, 23 reads: 'He who, seated as a neutral, is not moved by *gunas;* who, thinking that *gunas* act, is firm and moves not.'

3, 6. He who, restraining the organs of action, sits thinking in his mind of the objects of the senses, self-deluded, he is said to be one of false conduct.

In a word, a hypocrite. The organs of action are the hand, the foot, and so on. Stopping physical action while indulging in mental activity of the kind mentioned would be hypocritical.

3, 7. But whoso, restraining the senses by mind, O Arjuna, engages in Karma Yoga, unattached, with organs of action, he is esteemed.

The hypocrite of 3,6 is here contrasted with the Karma Yogin who performs actionless action, with the senses controlled. Verse 42 of discourse 3 says: 'They say that the senses are superior; superior to the senses is mind; superior to mind is reason; one who is even superior to reason is He.' 'He' is the Self (*Atman*).

3, 8. Do thou perform [thy] bounden duty; for, action is superior to inaction. And even the maintenance of the body would not be possible for thee by inaction.

3, 9. Except in the case of action for Sacrifice's sake, this world is action-bound. Action for the sake therefore, do thou, O son of Kunti, perform, free from attachment.

Maharishi Mahesh Yogi says that sacrifice (*yaghya*) should be given a broader meaning than religious ceremony, making it an action which aids evolution in the direction of higher consciousness. Worthwhile acts can also be viewed as devotional 'offerings'.

3, 19. Therefore, without attachment, constantly perform the action which should be done; for, performing action without attachment, man reaches the Supreme. . . .

3, 27. Actions are wrought in all cases by the energies of Nature. He whose mind is deluded by egoism thinks 'I am the doer'.

He who 'by egoism identifying the aggregate of the body and the senses with the Self, i.e., who ascribes to himself all the attributes of the body and the senses and thus thoroughly identifies himself with them – he, by nescience, sees actions in himself: as regards every action, he thinks "I am the doer".'

We have learned earlier that it is the three *gunas* that act and not the Self. The ego keeps thinking 'I' do this, 'I' do that. The ego bolsters its need for power by saying it acts, when lucid thought reveals that Nature (the interacting *gunas*) is responsible. Consider the meaning of saying 'I am hungry', 'I am angry', and so on. And ask yourself whether you breathe or are breathed.

3, 28. But he who knows the truth, O mighty-armed, about the divisions of the energies and [their] functions, is not attached, thinking that the energies act upon the energies.

'He who is versed in the classification of the energies [*gunas*] and their respective functions holds that the energies as sense-organs move amid the energies as sense-objects, but not the Self. Thus holding, he forms no attachments for actions'.

3, 30. Renouncing all actions in Me, with thy thought resting on the Self, being free from hope, free from selfishness, devoid of fever, do thou fight.

'Fever' here can mean anguish, grief, or delusion. Maharishi Mahesh Yogi translates (40): 'Surrendering all actions to Me by maintaining your consciousness in the Self, freed from longing and the sense of "mine", fight, delivered from the fever [of delusion].' To 'maintain your consciousness in the Self' while engaged in action requires an ability to retain the state of higher consciousness even in the market place and not just during the dive within in meditation. The Maharishi says:

Maintenance of transcendetal Self-consciousness along with activity in the waking state of consciousness requires co-existence of the two states of consciousness. The ability of man's nervous system, which is the physical machinery through which consciousness expresses itself, has to be developed to express these two states simultaneously. This is brought about by regularly interrupting the constant activity of the waking state of consciousness with periods of silence in transcendental consciousness. When, through this practice, the nervous system has been permanently conditioned to maintain these two states together, then the consciousness remains always centred in the Self. The Lord explains that this centering of consciousness in the Self is the way of 'surrendering all actions to Me.'

'All this is threaded on me,' says the *Gita*, 7, 7. We are one with the divine principle. Awareness of this on a plane of universal consciousness is the aim of all the Yogas. The Karma Yogin realizes it through selfless service, acting without thought for the fruits of action, non-grasping and non-clinging, his action a form of renunciation, devotion, and worship.

XII Yoga of Devotion: Bhakti

BHAKTI PRACTICE

Bhakti is the Way or Yoga of Devotion. Here again we have a form of meditation. Acts of devotion or adoration – in Hinduism, usually directed to chosen deities, Krishna being a favourite – should be performed in the meditative or contemplative manner: that is, the whole person wholly attending. For the Hindu, sincere devotion produces good *karmas*, and the Bhakti way merges naturally with that of Karma, the Yoga of Selfless Action. Devotion should be without egoism or expectation of rewards – petitioning God with prayers in the Christian manner is not customary. Bhakti thus fulfils the major purpose of all the esoteric Eastern psychologies, which is to dissovle the ego and to find the Self. Purification is an important feature of all Yoga practice. Here it is consciousness that is purified, the steady flame of Bhakti love burning up such spiritual impurities as hatred, anger, greed, pride, and other destructive emotions.

Bhakti makes a strong appeal to the Indian masses – it has always been their favourite Yoga. It requires simplicity of heart and a steady flow of devotion. It does not require education or a well-honed intellect; though, in the way that Yoga paths overlap, the intellectual approach does not exclude the worshipful: the two may work in harness.

But when not tempered by detachment and intellectual objectivity Bhakti adoration can pass into hysteria and possession. It then becomes the equivalent of the most emotional of the Christian sects: snake-handling, speaking with tongues, and the like occur. A report (10) on Bhakti worship and celebration in Bengal Vaishnaism lists the following behaviour observed as a result of arousing intense love of Krishna: '*nrtya* [dancing], *viluthita* [rolling on the ground], *gits* (singing), *krosana* [loud crying], *tanu-motana* [twisting of the body], *hujkara* [shouting], *jrmbha* [yawning], *svasa-bhuman* [profusion of sighs], *lokanapeksita* [disregard of popular opinion], *lalasrava* [foaming at the mouth], *atta-hasa* [loud laughter], *ghurna* [giddiness], *hikka* [hiccup].'

If adoration is steady it finds its own forms. Bhakti practice is an opening-up to the heart's will and direction. Worship takes different forms in different cultures. The Hindu expresses devotion in singing hymns of praise, in dancing, and in repeating (*japa*) *mantras.*

BHAKTI HYMNS

Bhakti songs of praise are often of lyric beauty, and are not without resemblances to Christian hymns.

The taming and steadying of the senses that is an important part of Yogic meditation is found in the following seventeenth-century Bhakti hymn by Tukaram (6):

THOUGH *HE* SLAY ME

Now I submit me to thy will,
Whether thou save or whether kill;
Keep thou near or send me hence,
Or plunge me in the war of sense.

Thee in my ignorance I sought,
Of true devotion knowing nought.
Little could I, a dullard, know,
Myself the lowest of the low.

My mind I cannot steadfast hold;
My senses wander uncontrolled.
Ah, I have sought and sought for peace.
In vain, for me there's no release.

Now bring I thee a faith complete
And lay my life before thy feet.
Do thou, O God, what seemeth best;
In thee, in thee alone is rest.

In thee I trust, and, hapless wight,
Cling to thy skirts with all my might.
My strength is spent, I, Tuka, say;
Now upon thee this task I lay.

Mahatma Gandhi was said to have a special affection for the following Vaishnavite hymn (10):

> He is the true Vaishnava who knows and feels another's woes as his own.
> Ever ready to serve, he never boasts.
> He bows to everyone, and despises no one, keeping his thought, word, and deed pure.
> Blessed is the mother of such an one. He reverences every woman as his mother.
> He keeps an equal mind and does not stain his lips with falsehood; nor does he touch another's wealth.
> No bonds of attachment can hold him.
> Ever in tune with Ramanama, his body possessed in itself all places of pilgrimage.
> Free from greed and deceit, passion and anger, this is the true Vaishnava.

MANTRAS

Bhakti employs concentrative meditation in repetition (*japa*) of *mantras*. 'The principle of *bhakti* is that the things we love and dwell upon we become,' says Ernest Wood (67).

> Hence the *mantras* of the gods and goddesses, who are powers and virtues are effective, as they are names. That is why people sing hymns, and why in Indian villages there is constantly the singing of songs with the repetitions of names or praises (*bhajans*) which are set to pleasing music relating the sound to the thought and to that extent forming a mental home or habitat where the mind can rest in an upward-turned condition.

He adds: 'With respect to every *mantra* – as in the case of Western ceremonial – there must be *intent*, otherwise the words of a parrot or of a gramophone would carry the full power.'

KRISHNA CONSCIOUSNESS

The Krishna Consciousness Movement, whose spiritual master is A. C. Bhaktivedanta Swami Prabhupada, is based on studying the Bhakti teachings of Lord Krishna in the *Bhagavad Gita* and on chanting the *mantra:* HARE KRISHNA, HARE KRISHNA, KRISHNA KRISHNA, HARE HARE, HARE RAMA, HARE RAMA, RAMA RAMA, HARE HARE. Young people dancing and chanting the preceding *mantra* have become a familiar sight in the major cities of the world.

Swami Prabhupada explains the purpose in chanting the *mantra* (49):

> What is ego? I am pure soul, but with my intelligence and mind I am in contact with matter, and I have identified myself with matter. This is false ego. I am pure soul, but I am identifying falsely. For example, I am identifying with the land, thinking that I am an Indian, or that I am American. This is called *ahamkara*. *Ahamkara* means the point where the pure soul touches matter. That junction is called *ahamkara*. *Ahamkara* is still finer than intelligence.
>
> Krishna says that these are the eight material elements: earth, water, fire, air, ether, mind, intelligence and false ego. False ego means false identification. Our nescient life has begun from this false identification – thinking that I am this matter, although I am seeing every day, at every moment, that I am not this matter. Soul is permanently existing, while matter is changing. This misconception, this illusion, is called *ahamkara* false ego. And your liberation means when you are out of this false ego. What is that status? *Aham brahmasmi*. I am *Brahman*, I am spirit. That is the beginning of liberation. . . .
>
> Simply understanding that I am not matter, I am soul, is not perfection. The impersonalist, the void philosopher, simply thinks of the negative, that I am not this matter, I am not this body. This will not stay. You have to not only realize that you are not matter, but you have to engage yourself in the spiritual world. And that spiritual world means to be working in Krishna consciousness. That spiritual world, that functioning of our real life, is Krishna consciousness.
>
> False ego I have already explained. It is neither matter nor spirit, but the junction – where the spirit soul comes into contact with matter and forgets himself. It is just as, in delirium, a man is diseased and his brain becomes puzzled, and gradually he forgets himself and becomes a madman. He is gradually forgetting. So there is the beginning of loss, and there is one point where he forgets. That beginning point is called *ahamkara*, or false ego.

Chanting the *mahamantra* – Hare Krishna, Hare Krishna, Krishna Krishna, Hare Hare, Hare Rama, Hare Rama, Rama Rama, Hare Hare – is the process not merely of putting an end to this false conception of the self, but it goes beyond that, to the point where the pure spirit soul engages in his eternal, blissful, all-knowing activities in the loving service of God. This is the height of conscious development, the ultimate goal of all living entities now evolving through the cycles and species of material nature.

Ahamkara is the 'I'-sense set up by the action of spirit on matter (*prakriti*). *Prakriti's* evolutes were discussed in the chapter entitled 'Yogic Philosophy.'

BHAKTI *SAMADHI*

Bhakti calls on the Raja Yoga techniques of concentration and contemplation – it cannot do otherwise if the devotional force is sincere and authentic. Its powerful content of love and unselfishness should also demand action and service to one's fellow men: that is, it should lead to working in harness with Karma Yoga. Concentration and contemplation can be sustained into *samadhi*. The *Gheranda Samhita* (61), one of the classic texts we consulted several times for *Yoga and Vitality*, describes Bhakti as one of the ways to Yoga's supreme goal of enlightenment- 'Let him contemplate within his heart his special Deity; let him be full of ecstasy by such contemplation; let him, with thrill, shed tears of happiness, and by so doing he will become entranced. This leads to *Samadhi* and *Manomani*.' *Manomani* is another word for *samadhi*.

Samadhi triggered by sustained emotional concentration in its initial stages will contain gross elements but, once established, can be purified and refined. The rapture of the Christian mystics often has this affective tone, for, like Bhakti, it is powered by personal devotion to God or to Christ. The ecstasy of St Teresa of Avila, which will be quoted in the chapter entitled 'Yoga of Sex: Tantrism', cannot be cited as a pure example of mystical illumination, for her experience clearly had a strong emotional, even erotic, content. The bliss of *samadhi* and its intuitive awareness are much finer, more lucid, and less supercharged.

D. T. Suzuji (59), who has done more than any other oriental to explain Zen Buddhism to the West, in one of his essays compares the affective tone of so much Christian mysticism with the impersonal tone of Eastern illumination – *samadhi* in Yoga, *satori* in Zen – and says that the emotional content is added by Christian doctrine and does not really belong to the universal experience.

> Perhaps the most remarkable aspect of the Zen experience is that it has no personal note in it as is observable in Christian mystic experiences.

There is no reference whatever in Buddhist *satori* to such personal and frequently sexual feelings and relationships as are to be gleaned from these terms: flame of love, a wonderful love shed in the heart, embrace, the beloved, bride, bridegroom, spiritual matrimony, Father, God, the Son of God, God's child, etc. We may say that all these terms are interpretations based on a definite system of thought and really have nothing to do with the experience itself. At any rate, alike in India, China, and Japan, *satori* has remained thoroughly impersonal, or rather highly intellectual.

Bhakti, however, is the Yoga with the strongest affective tone, though it is true to say that Bhakti *samadhi* is not so emotional as the experiences related by some of the Christian mystics. But Christian mystics vary in temperament: Meister Eckhart is clearly intellectual (a Jnana Yogin), and St John of the Cross (St Teresa's compatriot) blends harmoniously two paths to illumination: love and understanding.

CHRISTIAN YOGAS

Bhakti and Christian worship have affinities: both direct devotion and adoration to divine figures. A little thought will show that Christianity, like Hinduism, has its Bhakti, Karma, and Jnana paths – those of devotion, social service, and intellection respectively. It has its Mantra Yoga in prayer, its Raja Yoga in meditation and contemplation. Only Hatha Yoga, with its physical exercises and breath controls, fails to find a correspondence. (The English emphasis on building moral fibre on the playing fields points in that direction, but is only faintly comparable.)

THE *GITA* ON BHAKTI YOGA

Bhakti Yogins have a special affection for the *Bhagavad Gita*, in particular those chapters which describe the Yoga of Devotion. Discourses 9 to 12 are mainly devotional – Discourse 12 is an account of Bhakti Yoga. Devotion to the Supreme is described in the following verses:

9, 18. I am the Goal, the Sustainer, the Lord, the Witness, the Abode, the Shelter and the Friend, the Origin, Dissolution and Stay; the Treasure-house, the Seed imperishable.

9, 22. Those men who, meditating on Me as non-separate, worship Me all around – to them who are ever devout, I secure gain and safety.

9, 26. When one offers to Me with devotion a leaf, a flower, a fruit, water – that I eat, offered with devotion by the pure-minded.

9, 27. Whatever thou doest, whatever thou eatest, whatever thou sacrificest, whatever thou givest, in whatever austerity thou engagest, do it as an offering to Me.

9, 28. Thus shalt thou be liberated from the bonds of actions which are productive of good and evil results; equipped in mind with the Yoga of renunciation, and liberated, thou shalt come to Me.

9, 34. Fix thy mind on Me, be devoted to Me, sacrifice to Me, bow down to Me. Thus steadied, with Me as thy Supreme Goal, thou shalt reach Myself, the Self.

'Steadied' in the above verse refers to keeping the pool of mind-stuff (*citta*) unruffled. 'The Self' refers to the Self of all beings. And Self equals Cosmic Self.

10, 20. I am the Self, O Gudakesa, seated in the heart of all beings; I am the beginning and the middle, as also the end, of all beings.

Sankaracharya, the most illustrious commentator on the *Gita*, considered the following verse to be 'the essence of the whole teaching . . . which conduces to Highest Bliss':

11, 55. He who does work for Me, who looks on Me as the Supreme, who is devoted to Me, who is free from attachment, who is without hatred for any being, he comes to Me, O Pandava.

Verses 13 to 20 of Discourse 12 are cherished by Bahkti Yogins:

12, 13-14. He who hates no single being, who is friendly and compassionate to all, who is free from attachment and egoism, to whom pain and pleasure are equal, who is enduring, ever content and balanced in mind, self-controlled, and possessed of firm conviction, whose thought and reason are directed to Me, he who is [thus] devoted to Me is dear to Me.

12, 15. He by whom the world is not afflicted and who is not afflicted by the world, who is free from joy, envy, fear and sorrow, he is dear to Me.

12, 16. He who is free from wants, who is pure, clever, unconcerned, untroubled, renouncing all undertakings, he who is [thus] devoted to Me is dear to Me.

12, 17. He who neither rejoices, nor hates, nor grieves, nor desires, renouncing good and evil, he who is full of devotion is dear to Me.

12, 18-19. He who is the same to foe and friend, and also in honour and dishonour; who is the same in cold and heat, in pleasure and pain; who is free from attachment; to whom censure and praise are equal; who is silent, content with anything, homeless, steady-minded, full of devotion; that man is dear to Me.

12, 20. They, verily, who follow this immortal Law described above, endued with faith, looking up to Me as the Supreme, and devoted, they are exceedingly dear to Me.

Sir Edwin Arnold's verse translation of the *Bhagavad Gita* presents the final lines of Discourse 12 less literally than the translation given above, but more poetically:

Who fixed in faith on me
Dotes upon none, scorns none; rejoices not,
And grieves not, letting good or evil hap
Light when it will, and when it will depart,
That man I love! Who, unto friend and foe
Keeping an equal heart, with equal mind
Bears shame and glory; with an equal peace
Takes heat and cold, pleasure and pain; abides
Quit of desires, hears praise or calumny
In passionless restraint, unmoved by each;
Linked by no ties to earth, steadfast in Me,
That Man I love!

XIII Yoga of Knowledge: Jnana

REASON AND BEYOND

Just as Karma Yoga is the way of action and Bhakti Yoga the way of devotion, so Jnana Yoga is the way of knowledge. It does not exclude assistance from other Yogas, but in itself stands out because it makes use of conscious reasoning to penetrate the veils of ignorance and illusion that prevent our seeing the light of that pure consciousness which Yogins consider the basis of life and its secret. But intellectual understanding needs to be reinforced by the experience of meditation in which thought is transcended because the meditator has gone to its source within.

Jnana Yoga uses the well-honed intellect to cut a way through the tangle of mental impressions (*samskaras*) to find the truth that dwells in the place the *upanishads* call 'the space within the heart'.

The English poet Robert Browning wrote, in 'Paracelsus':

> Truth is within ourselves; it takes no rise
> From outward things, whate'er you may believe.
> There is an inmost centre in us all,
> Where truth abides in fullness; and around,
> Wall upon wall, the gross flesh hems it in,
> This perfect, clear perception – which is truth.
> A baffling and perverting carnal mesh
> Binds it, and makes all error: and, to *know*
> Rather consists in opening out a way
> Whence the imprisoned spendour may escape,
> Than in effecting entry for a light
> Supposed to be without.

The Jnana Yogin uses the penetrating power of thought to open out a way to the 'inmost centre', but in the end thought is stilled, falls silent, and is transcended. It is not a question of despising or underestimating the powers of reason, but of taking them as far as they will go, which is to the taking-off point for transcendental consciousness, sometimes called bliss consciousness (*sat chit ananda*).

The greatest Yoga teachers look on Yoga as a science that does not contradict reason, though in the final stage it goes beyond it to the plane of Being. Swami Vivekananda taught that the lower and higher stages of consciousness belong to the same mind and that Yogic Enlightenment fulfils reason. This is how he put it (64):

> To get any reason out of the mass of incongruity we call human life, we have to transcend our reason, but we must do it scientifically, slowly, by regular practice, and we must cast off all superstition. We must take up the study of the super-conscious state just as any other science. On reason we must lay our foundation, we must follow reason as far as it leads; and when reason fails, reason itself will show us the way to the highest plane. When you hear a man say, 'I am inspired', and then talk irrationally, reject it. Why? Because these three states – instinct, reason and super-consciousness, or the unconscious, conscious, and super-conscious states – belong to one and the same mind. There are three minds in one man, but one state of it develops into the others. Instinct develops into reason, and reason into the transcendental consciousness; therefore not one of the states contradicts the others. Real inspiration never contradicts reason, but fulfils it. Just as you find the great prophets saying, 'I come not to destroy but to fulfil', so inspiration always comes to full reason, and is in harmony with it.

Vivekananda is repeating a teaching expressed in the sixth century BC in the *Bhagavad Gita*:

> 3, 42. They say that the senses are superior; superior to the sense is mind; superior to mind is reason; one who is even superior to reason is He.

The distinction made in Yoga between mind (*manas*), which is concerned with selection and rejection, assimilation and co-ordination, and reason or intellect (*buddhi*) is here brought out. The latter is higher than the former in the evolution towards Self-realization. Sankaracharya, the leading expounder of Jnana Yoga, comments on the above verse (54):

> The senses are five, the sense of hearing, etc. When compared with the physical body, which is gross, external, and limited, the senses are superior as they are comparatively more subtle and internal, and have a more extensive sphere of action. So say the wise. Superior to the senses is mind (*manas*, the impulsive nature) which is composed of

thoughts and desires, of errors and doubts (*sankalpa* and *vikalpa*). Superior to mind is reason (*buddhi*) characterized by determination (*nischaya*). So, He who is behind all things visible, inclusive of reason, the Dweller in the body, whom – it has been said – desire, seated in the senses and other quarters, bewilders by enveloping wisdom – He, the Self, the witness of reason, is superior to reason.

The concluding verse of Discourse 3 follows:

3, 43. Thus knowing Him who is superior to reason, subduing the self by the self, slay thou, O mighty-armed, the enemy in the form of desire, hard to conquer.

Lord Krishna is instructing the young warrior Arjuna. Understanding the Self, the *Atman* which is identical with the Absolute One or *Brahman*, is the heart of Jnana Yoga practice and experience.

REGRESSION OR EVOLUTIONARY ADVANCE?

The Western rationalist is wary of going beyond reason. He may also suspect that the superconscious state of mystical experience is a regression to primitive or fetal levels of existence. Sigmund Freud and other psycho-analysts have taken this view. Those Yogins who have attained Self-realization (*samadhi*) aver that the mystic experience is not a regression but an evolutionary advance based on an integration that is the highest possible development of human consciousness, in which the subject-object duality is reconciled in a new unity which is the essence of maturity.

Professor Eliade puts the case for the goal of Yogic meditation, Patanjali's eighth and final stage (18):

It would b a gross error to regard this supreme reintegration as a mere regression to primordial nondistinction. It can never be repeated too often that Yoga, like many other mysticisms, issues on the plane of paradox and not on a commonplace and easy extinction of consciousness. As we shall see, from time immemorial India has known the many and various trances and ecstasies obtained from intoxicants, narcotics, and all the other elementary means of emptying consciousness; but any degree of methodological conscience will show us that we have no right to put *samadhi* among these countless varieties of spiritual escape. Liberation is not assimilable with the 'deep sleep' of prenatal existence, even if the recovery of totality through undifferentiated enstasis seems to resemble the bliss of the human being's fetal preconsciousness. One essential fact must always be borne in mind: the yogin works on all levels of consciousness and of the subconscious, for the purpose of opening the way to transconsciousness (knowledge-possession of the Self, the *purusa*). He enters into 'deep sleep' and into the 'fourth state' (*turiya*, the cataleptic state) with the utmost lucidity; he does not sink into self-hypnosis. The importance that all authors ascribe to the yogic states of *super*consciousness shows us that the final reintegration takes place in *this* direction, and not in a trance, however profound. In other words: the recovery, through *samadhi*, of the initial nonduality introduces a new element in comparison with the primordial situation (that which existed before the twofold division of the real into object-subject). That element is *knowledge* of unity and bliss. There is a 'return to the beginning,' but with the difference that the man 'liberated in this life' recovers the original situation enriched by the dimensions of *freedom* and *transconsciousness*.

THE ONION GAME

Though the mystic experience is ineffable and can only be known by direct experience, nevertheless mystics sometimes feel drawn to attempt a negative description: if they cannot say what it is, they can at least say what it is not, the Hindu 'not this, not that' (*neti, neti*). And they continue the stripping process until nothing remains, or rather Nothing, for we speak now of what Buddhists call the Void, which is really a plenitude and the source of every manifest thing. Other names the experience goes by are Being, Self, Ultimate Reality, *Brahman*, *Atman*, Cosmic Consciousness, God, Godhead.

The *Tao Te Ching* says in its opening line: 'The Tao that can be expressed is not the eternal Tao.' And St John of the Cross speaks for all mystics when he says (30):

> We receive this mystical knowledge of God [Being, Self, etc.] clothed in none of the kinds of images, in none of the sensible representations which our mind makes use of in other circumstances. Accordingly in this knowledge, since the senses and imagination are not employed, we get neither form nor impression, nor can we give any account or furnish any likeness, although the mysterious and sweet tasting wisdom comes here so directly to the innermost parts of the soul.

Father Augustin Baker (1575-1641), in one of his many treatises on the prayer of contemplation, states (2):

> By reason of this habituation and absolute dominion of the Holy Spirit

in the souls of the perfect (who have wholly neglected, forgotten, and lost themselves, to the end that God alone may live in them, whom they contemplate in the absolute obscurity of faith), hence it is that some mystic writers do call this perfect union the UNION OF NOTHING WITH NOTHING, that is, the union of the soul, which is nowhere corporally, that hath no images nor affections to creatures in her; yes, that hath lost the free disposal of her own faculties, acting by a portion of the spirit above all the faculties, and according to the actual touches of the Divine Spirit, and apprehending God with an exclusion of all conceptions and apprehensions; thus it is that the soul, being nowhere corporally or sensibly, is everywhere spiritually and immediately united to God, this infinite nothing.

A stripping away ('not this, not that') is basic to the meditative practice of the Jnana Yogin in answer to the key question: Who (or what) am I? Like so many onion skins, the 'not I' things are peeled away, until the last skin is discarded and only the fullness of Being remains. The goal of the Onion Game has then been reached. Any person can play, though the game suits the intellectual temperament, just as Bhakti Yoga suits the devotional temperament and Karma Yoga the active temperament.

Sufis are taught to pursue the 'Who am I?' inquiry in this meditation:

I am not the body.
I am not the senses.
I am not the mind.
I am not this.
I am not that.
What then am I? What is the Self?
It is in the body.
It is in everybody.
It is everywhere.
It is the All.
It is Self. I am It. Absolute oneness.

Sufism is the mystical wing of the Islamic religion. The Sufic final stage of *fana* or 'passing away' has close affinities with the Hindu *samadhi* and the Buddhist *nirvana*. Among the various mystical traditions, descriptions of stages of the 'way' parallel each other to a considerable extent, and the final stage is inevitably a transcending of the ego and a finding of the Self.

THE *CHANDOGYA UPANISHAD*

The oldest extant accounts of how to play the Onion Game are those of the *upanishads*, notably the *Chandogya Upanishad*, which is amongst the earliest. It is believed that the first *upanishads* were written about 800 BC. These metaphysical treatises, which instruct in Yoga, are mostly the records of schools of wisdom centred on forest sages – in a sense, school notes. A few of the sages' names are mentioned, but the majority remain anonymous.

The central teaching, expressed again and again using a variety of analogies, is the *raison d'être* of Yoga practice – the *Atman* (Self) within is one with *Brahman*, the subtle essence of all things. 'That thou art' (*tatatvam asi*).

In the *Chandogya Upanishad* Svetaketu, who is twenty-four years old and has studied for twelve years, has still to learn the fundamental message about Self and the All from his father (6, 12-13, translated by Max Muller):

'Fetch me from thence a fruit of the Nyagrodha tree.'

'Here is one, Sir,'

'Break it.'

'It is broken, Sir.'

'What do you see there?'

'These seeds, almost infinitesimal.'

'Break one of them.'

'It is broken, Sir.'

'What do you see there?'

'Not anything, Sir.'

The father said: 'My son, that subtile essence which you do not perceive there, of that very essence this great Nyagrodha tree exists.

'Believe it, my son. That which is the subtle essence, in it all that exists has its self. It is the True. It is the Self, and thou, O Svetaketu, art it.'

'Please, Sir, inform me still more,' said the son.

'Be it so, my child,' the father replied.

'Place this salt in water, and wait on me in the morning.'

The son did as he was commanded.

The father said to him: 'Bring me the salt, which you placed in the water last night.'

The son having looked for it, found it not, for, of course, it was melted.

The father said: 'Taste it from the surface of the water. How is it?'

The son replied: 'It is salt.'

'Taste it from the middle. How is it?'

The son replied: 'Is is salt.'

The father said: 'Throw it away and then wait on me.'

He did so; but salt exists for ever.

Then the father said: 'Here also, in this body, forsooth, you do not perceive the True (*sat*), my son; but there indeed it is.

'That which is the subtle essence, in it all that exists has its self. It is true. It is the Self, and thou, O Svetaketu, art it.'

In section 8 of the *Chandogya Upanishad* there is a long account of meditation in pursuit of the Self – 'I am not this, I am not that' The teacher is Prajapati, and his pupil is the god Indra. Here is Prajapati's concluding instruction, in the translation of Juan Mascaro (43):

It is true that the body is mortal, that it is under the power of death; but it is also the dwelling of *Atman*, the Spirit of immortal life. The body, the house of the Spirit, is under the power of pleasure and pain; and if a man is ruled by his body then this man can never be free. But when a man is in the joy of the Spirit, in the spirit which is ever free, then this man is free from all bondage, the bondage of pleasure and pain.

The wind has not a body, nor lightning, nor thunder, nor clouds; but when those rise into the higher spheres then they find their body of light. In the same way, when the soul is in silent quietness it arises and leaves the body, and reaching the Spirit Supreme finds there its body of light. It is the land of infinite liberty where, beyond its mortal body, the Spirit of man is free. There can he laugh and sing of his glory with ethereal women and friends. He enjoys ethereal chariots and forgets the cart of his body on earth. For as a beast is attached to a cart, so on earth the soul is attached to a body.

'Know that when the eye looks into space it is the Spirit of man that sees: the eye is only the organ of sight. When one says "I feel this perfume', it is the Spirit that feels: he uses the organ of smell. When one says 'I am speaking', it is the Spirit that speaks: the voice is the organ of speech. When one says 'I am hearing', it is the Spirit that hears: the ear is the organ of hearing. And when one says 'I think', it is the Spirit that thinks: the mind is the organ of thought. It is because of the light of the Spirit that the human mind can see, and can think, and enjoy this world.

'All the gods in the heaven of *Brahman* adore in contemplation their

Infinite Spirit Supreme. This is why they have all joy, and all the worlds and all desires. And the man who on this earth finds and knows *Atman*, his own Self, has all his holy desires and all the worlds and all joy.'

I AM

Patanjali named certain *klesas* (afflictions) that the Yogin needs to eliminate. They are metaphysical ignorance (*avidya*), not recognizing one's real nature, confusion as to the nature of Reality, identifying with the ego, the sense of I-am-ness (*asmita*), attractions and repulsions, the desire for life or death. The root *klesa* is *avidya*, the ignorance responsible for our bondage, the spirit's imprisonment in matter. Patanjali defines *asmita* as a mixing of pure consciousness (*purusha*) and cognition (*buddhi*). However, it is not the pure 'I am' that is the trouble, but wrong identification with its enmeshment in matter.

Thus a modern commentator on Patanjali's *Yoga Sutras* writes (60):

> 'I am' represents the pure awareness of self-existence and is therefore the expression . . . of pure consciousness or the *purusha*. When the pure consciousness gets involved in matter and, owing to the power of *maya*, knowledge of its real nature is lost, the pure 'I am' changes into 'I am this', where 'this' may be the subtlest vehicle through which it is working, or the grossest vehicle, namely, the physical body. The two processes – namely, the loss of awareness of its real nature and the identification with the vehicles – are simultaneous.

Note Exodus 3: 14: 'And God said unto Moses, I AM THAT I AM: and he said, Thus shalt thou say unto the children of Israel, I AM hath sent me unto you.'

I AM experience is the *purusha* or *atman* of the Yogin. It is the Self beyond the ego, and the constant behind the changes of body, intellect, and feeling.

THE ELUSIVE *I*

Look within for your *I*. It is more elusive than the Scarlet Pimpernel. We seek it here, we seek it there – but each time it eludes your grasp by becoming the *I* of a moment ago in an infinite regression. This *I* is not the contents of consciousness, for they can become the objects of consciousness at any moment. Who then observes the contents of the mind? Observing the mind you see objects of consciousness but not consciousness itself. Introspective self-examination is always the study of things of the past, even when that past is just a moment ago. And if we identify the *I* with our thoughts, images, and emotions, then we make the disconcerting discovery that we are not a single *I* but a multiplicity of *I's* each, in P. D. Ouspensky's phrase, seeking to be caliph, for an hour, sometimes only for a minute.

Some of the great Western philosophers have been puzzled by their inability to locate or grasp the elusive *I*. 'I can never catch my *self*,' said David Hume, 'Whenever I try, I always stumble at some sense-impression or idea.' And William James said: 'The so-called "self" is only a stream of thought; the passing thought itself is the thinker.' Jean-Paul Sartre too, has played the Onion Game, coming up with a concept of man's radical 'freedom' that is an existentialist version of Yoga's *moksha*. Again, Sartre's concept that man as Being-for-itself – in contrast to Being-in-itself (such as rocks, trees, and clouds) – brings Nothingness into the world has affinities with Hindu and Buddhist ideas of the Void. Hazel Barnes (3), a lucid interpreter of Sartre's philosophy, here shows how the French philosopher answers the key question of Jnana Yoga: 'Who (or What) am I?'

> If I probe inward to find out what I really am, the only demonstrable objective unity I can discover is inextricably bound up with my autobiography. Yet I feel that this accumulated essence is too inert to be that directing consciousness which projects itself towards the future. I sense confusedly that the subject consciousness cannot be identified without any given set of attitudes; yet I remain convinced that throughout my psychic experience there is some transcendent unity, something which is involved in every state of consciousness without being restricted to any one of them. The mystery is explained by Sartre's conclusion that each consciousness is particular but not personal. The personal ego is on the side of the psychic; that is, it belongs with all the psychological phenomena which we view objectively as the personality. But the personality is not a structure of consciousness in the sense that we might describe the makeup of an optical lens. It is that at which the lens is directed. Consciousness itself is not timid

or courageous or avaricious or generous. These qualities exist *for* consciousness. It evokes them, brings them into the world, for others and for itself. . . .

The unity of my psychic life lies precisely in my accumulation of psychic experience. The 'I' and the 'Me' are respectively the active and passive ideal poles of all that I have experienced and will experience. Therefore, the feeling of frustration which comes over me when I try introspectively to find myself reflects exactly what I actually am. If I seek to find an 'I' endowed with personal qualities, I can find one objectively in my psychic history, but the 'I' is always in the past or, by imagination, in the future. The consciousness which continues to produce it is without personal qualities. Thus my dim comprehension that the active source of my awareness trascends any 'I' which even the most accurate self-analysis could evoke is exactly correct.

If consciousness stands aloof even from the personality, it is determined by nothing save itself. Here is the source of Sartre's radical freedom. My consciousness is not myself. . . .

Granted that this self-consciousness is impersonal, what *is* it? . . . Even if we are to say that the self-consciousness is not personal, it seems that it must be something or there could be no sense of self. Or if consciousness is process and not entity, of what is it a process? I am not sure that Sartre could – or would – claim that he could give a totally satisfactory answer to that basic question. This is partly because to do so would involve us in purely metaphysical speculations which seek to go behind reality.

At the crucial point Sartre draws back from metaphysics and the numinous, not acknowledging anything holy or worthy of worship in the pure consciousness uncovered by the stripping power of his intellect. Nor does he look at meditation as a technique for exploring consciousness and going 'behind reality'.

IN PURSUIT OF THE *I*

The climax of Dr Paul Brunton's *A Search in Secret India* (7) comes when he receives this instruction from a Maharishi:

'Pursue the enquiry "Who am I?" relentlessly. Analyse your entire personality. Try to find out where the I-thought begins. Go on with your meditations. Keep turning your attention within. One day the wheel of thought will slow down and an intuition will mysteriously arise. Follow that intuition, let your thinking stop, and it will eventually lead you to the goal.'

Dr Brunton gave an account of 'Who am I?' meditation in the *The Quest of the Overself* (8), published three years after *A Search in Secret India*.

An unorthodox account of playing the Onion Game is that given by Aubrey Menen in the concluding pages of his autobiography *The Space Within The Heart* (45). Mr Menen, the son of an Indian father and an Irish mother, tells how he isolated himself in a small room in the heart of the Thieves' Quarter of Rome and proceeded to examine his life, shedding layer after layer of his personality after holding each up to the light of his attention. Basing the stripping of his conditioned ego skins on the method taught in the *upanishads*, Mr Menen finally reached what that work calls 'the space within the heart'. It is here that he is most challenging and unorthodox:

'The philosophers of the *Upanishads*, after having led the reader into the very depths of his being, with shattering results to all his dearest beliefs, advise him to get up and go and enjoy himself like anybody else, with, they specify, horses, chariots, food and women. The verses in which this is said are as coarse as a hearty laugh and a slap on the back. How people manage to find God in such a book I cannot say, but I think it may be that they have a natural refinement which puts things decently straight.'

One may assume that Aubrey Menen would attribute Juan Mascaro's repeated use of the qualifying adjective 'ethereal' in the extract from the *Chandogya Upanishad* given earlier in this chapter, and his use of 'soul' rather than 'Self', to the 'natural refinement which puts things decently straight'.

Aubrey Menen returned to what he holds to be the unadulterated message of the *upanishads* in his book The New Mystics (44), published four years after his autobiography. He says that a 'gigantic fig-leaf' has been spread over the direct and simple teachings of the *upanishads*. He describes the Onion Game again, stressing the need for shedding the layers of personality put there by parents, teachers, and society. (A similar teaching of the necessity of not identifying the Self with our conditioned ideas, attitudes, and memories may be found in the books and recorded talks of Jiddu Krishnamurti).

'Disembodied laughter' is the nearest Mr Menen feels he can get to describing the feeling of being in 'the space within the heart' (45). 'Then a great tranquillity steals over you. It trickles like water through the cells of your mind, washing them clean. You think of nothing, nothing at all, but with a crystalline awareness, and it is the end of your search.'

Yogins call this centre of consciousness the Self or Atman. And to know the *Atman* is to know *Brahman*, which is the ground of all Being.

XIV Psychic Powers (Siddhis)

THE CORRECT ATTITUDE FOR YOGINS

Told that another Yogi master had walked across the waters of a broad and deep river, a famous Tibetan Yogi retorted: 'His feat wasn't worth the penny it would have cost him to take the ferry.' This attitude to occult powers is taken by the most respected Yoga masters, and by Patanjali in his *Yoga Sutras*, in which he lists the psychic attainments (*siddhis*) resulting from the Yoga of Meditation, but points out that they are obstacles in the way of attainment of Self-realization, Yoga's goal.

Possession of psychic powers, when made the primary aim of mastering the internal nature, leads to ego-inflation. Patanjali, and other authorities, therefore say that such awakened powers should be treated in a matter-of-fact manner, as extensions of the ordinary senses, and not allowed to become distractions from the goal of stilling the mind and uncovering the pure Self. Nor should telepathy, clairvoyance, or any such attainments be used for worldly ends. Patanjali says that *siddhis* can be produced by means other than meditation: by drugs, fasting, and incantations (*mantras*), for example. A few people are born with them.

A wide range of psychic powers is listed by Patanjali in Section 3 of the *Yoga Sutras*. These are variously interpreted, from a fundamentalist approach that believes in them literally to the viewpoint that every one of them should be taken symbolically. It should also be mentioned that Yoga meditation and respiratory control can induce the feelings that the body has shrunk to minute size, that it has become light as air, that it is floating, and so on.

PATANJALI'S LISTING OF PSYCHIC ATTAINMENTS

Patanjali listed various powers which arise when *samyama* – that is, concentration, contemplation, *samadhi* – is applied to certain things. It should be recalled that there is a qualitative change in *samyama* from the gross to the subtle.

3, 16. The knowledge of past and future, by *Samyama* on the three transformations.

The three transformations are 'property, character, and condition' (according to Dvivedi), or 'form, time, and state,' (according to Vivekananda).

3, 17. The word, its sense, and knowledge, are confused with one another on account of their being mutually mistaken for one another; hence by *Samyama* on the proper province of each [arises] the comprehension of [the meaning of] sounds uttered by any being.

3, 18. By mental presentation of the impressions, a knowledge of former class.

Vivekananda translates this as 'former life'.

3, 19. With reference to a sign, the knowledge of the mind of others.

3, 20. But not with its occupant, for that is not the subject.

'But not its contents', says Vivekananda.

3, 21. By *Samyama* on the form of the body, the power of comprehension being suspended, and the connection between light and eye being severed, there follows disappearance of the body.

3, 22. *Karma* is of two kinds: active and dormant. By *Samyama* on them [results] knowledge of cessation; as also by portents.

'Cessation' here means death.

3, 23. In sympathy, etc., strength.

By making *samyama* on sympathy, friendship, mercy, and so on, comes a strengthening of these qualities.

3, 24. In strength, that of the elephant, etc.

3, 25. The knowledge of the subtile, the obscure, and the remote, by contemplation of the inner light.

3, 26. By *Samyama* on the sun, the knowledge of space.

Vivekananda translates 'the knowledge of the world':

3, 27. In the moon, the knowledge of the starry regions.

3, 28. In the pole-star, knowledge of their motions.

That is, the motions of the stars.

3, 29. In the navel-circle, the knowledge of the arrangement of the body.

This refers to the subtle body and its energy centres (*chakras*), energy channels (*nadis*), and so on.

3, 30. In the pit of the throat, the cessation of hunger and thirst.

Compare this with the *Siva Samhita:* (64) 'Let the Yogi seat himself in the *Padmasana* [Lotus Posture] and fix his attention on the cavity of the throat, let him place his tongue at the base of the palate; by this he will extinguish hunger and thirst.'

3, 31. In the *Kurma-nadi*, steadiness.

Again compare this with the *Siva Samhita:* (64) 'Below the cavity of the throat, there is a beautiful *Nadi* [vessel] called *Kurma:* when the Yogi fixes his attention on it, he acquires great concentration of the thinking principle [*citta*[.' Vivekananda translates this as 'fixity of body', not thought.

3, 32. In the light of the head, the sight of the *Siddhis.*

The *Siva Samhita* says (62): 'When the Yogi constantly thinks he has got a third eye – the eye of Siva – in the middle of his forehead, he then perceives a fire, brilliant like lightning. By contemplating on this light, all sins are destroyed, and even the most wicked person obtains the highest end. If the experienced Yogi thinks of this light day and night he sees *Siddhas* [adepts], and can certainly converse with them.'

3, 33. Or everything from the result of *Pratibha* [intuition].

3, 34. In the heart, knowledge of mind.

3, 35. Experience is the indistinctness of the mild conception of *Sattva* and *Purusha* which are absolutely apart; this enjoyment being for another, knowledge of *Purusha* arises from *Samyama* on himself.

3, 36. Thence is produced intuitional [cognition of] sound, touch, sight, taste, and smell.

It is at this point that Patanjali interpolates the admonition mentioned in the opening paragraph of this chapter:

3, 37. These are obstacles in the way of *Samadhi*, and are powers in moments of suspension.

The *Tattva-vaisaradi* of Vacaspati Misra (about 850 AD) comments (57): 'It is only he whose mind is active in going out that becomes proud of the possession of these as attainments. A beggar in life may think that the possession of a little wealth is the fullness of riches. The yogi, however, who is inclined to the attainment of trance [*samadhi*] must reject them whenever they come.'

3, 38. The mind enters another body, by relaxation of the cause of bondage, and by knowledge of the method of passing.

3, 39. By mastery over *Udana*, ascension, and non-contact with water, mud, thorns, and so on.

By gaining control over the energy current called *udana* within the subtle body a Yogi can cross rivers without paying a penny to the ferryman, walk with bare feet on thorns, and so on.

3, 40. Effulgence by mastery over *samana*.

Samana is a subtle energy current that operates between the pelvis and the navel.

3, 41. By *Samyama* on the relation between *akasa* and the sense of hearing, [arises] supernatural audition.

Akasa is space.

3, 42. By *Samyama* on the relation between the body and *akasas*, as also by being identified with light [things like] cotton, [there follows] passage through space.

Vyasa (fourth century AD) comments (57): 'Wherever there is the body, there is the *akasa*. The body becomes related to the *akasa*, because the latter gives room to the former. Having mastered the relation by the attainment of the state of thought transforming into light things such as cotton, etc., down to the atom, the yogi becomes light. Thence does he get the power of roaming through space and walking over water with his feet. He walks over a spider's web, and then walks over the rays of light. Then does he get the power of roaming through space at will.'

3, 43. The external, unthought-of transformation [of the mind] is the great incorporeal; hence the destruction of the covering of illumination.

3, 44. Mastery over the elements, by *Samyama* on the gross, the constant, the subtile, the all-pervading, and the fruition-bearing [in them].

Vivekananda comments (64): 'By making *Samyama* on the gross and fine forms of the elements, their essential traits, the inheritance of the *Gunas* in them and on their contributing to the experience of the soul, comes mastery of the elements.'

3, 45. Then the attainment of *anima* and others, as also of perfection of the body and the corresponding non-obstruction of its functions.

'*Anima* and others' refers to eight attainments, said also to result from mastery of *pranayama*. They are:

i *Anima :* to become as small as an atom
ii *Mahima :* to become very large
iii *Laghima :* to become very light

iv *Garima*: to become very heavy
v *Prapti*: to be able to go anywhere
vi *Prakamya*: to have one's desires fulfilled.
vii *Vashitva*: to control all nature
viii *Ishitva*: to possess the power to create.

3, 46. Beauty gracefulness, strength, adamantine hardness, constitute perfection of the body.

3, 47. Mastery over the organs of sense by *Samyama* on the power of cognition, nature, egoism, all-pervasiveness, and fruition-giving capacity [of them].

3, 48. Thence fleetness [as of] mind, the being unobstructed by instruments, and complete mastery over the *pradhana*.

Pradhana is the first cause, the root of all – another name for *prakriti*.

3, 49. In him who is fixed upon the distinctive relation of *sattva* and *Purusha* [arise] mastery over all things and the knowledge of all.

3, 50. By non-attachment even thereto, follows *Kaivalya*, the seeds of bondage being destroyed.

Kaivalya is absolute independence and freedom. It is the subject-matter of Section 4 of Patanjali's *Yoga Sutras*.

3, 51. [There should be] entire destruction of pleasure and pride in the invitations by the powers [of various places], for there is possibility of a repetition of evil.

3, 52. Discriminative knowledge from *Samadhi* on moments. Their order.

3, 53. From it knowledge of similars, there being non-discrimination by class, characteristic, or position.

3, 54. The knowledge born of discrimination to *taraka*, relating to all objects, in every condition, and simultaneous.

Taraka is the highest knowledge possible to a Yogin.

3, 55. *Kaivalya* on the equality of purity between *Purusha* and *sattva*.

EXTRAORDINARY SENSE-PERCEPTIONS

In Section 1, *sutra* 35 Patanjali refers to 'forms of concentration that bring extraordinary sense-perceptions'. He adds that these encourage Yogins to persist with their meditation.

Swami Vivekananda commented on this (64):

This naturally comes with Dharana, concentration; the Yogis say, if the mind becomes concentrated on the tip of the nose, one begins to smell, after a few days, wonderful perfumes. If it becomes concentrated at the root of the tongue, one begins to hear sounds; if on the tip of the tongue, one begins to taste wonderful flavours; if on the middle of the tongue, one feels as if he were coming in contact with something. If one concentrates his mind on the palate he begins to see peculiar things. If a man whose mind is disturbed wants to take some of these practices of Yoga, yet doubts the truth of them, he will have his doubts set at rest when, after a little practice, these things come to him, and he will persevere.

XV Yoga of Sex: Tantrism

YOGA AND SEXUAL ENERGY

A living Indian tradition, of ancient origin, aims at harnessing the great forces of sexual energy for the purpose of achieving higher consciousness. This tradition is divided into two contrasting ways of utilizing sexual power.

The first achieves its effects by concentrating and conserving sexual energy by chastity without repression. The celibacy a *guru* demands of his pupil (*chela*) is to conserve energy and to avoid distractions that could mar the single-mindedness and concentration required in Yogic disciplines. It has nothing to with a sense of guilt, shame, sin, or disgust in connection with sex. On the contrary, the sexual energies (even sexual fluid) are to be hoarded as though they were gold. And the reasons for celibacy are ascetic only in the original meaning of the word: *askesis* was the discipline voluntarily undergone by the Greek athlete in strict training.

The second approach sees in sexual union itself the means of expanding consciousness. Coitus becomes sacramental, an act of contemplation. It may be actual or imaginative; orgasm may or may not occur.

The married 'householder' Yogin (*grihastha*) is free to draw on both ways of harnessing sexual energy. He may choose chastity at times to focus the libido for spiritual ends, and at other times he will deepen sexual relations with his wife in the spirit of Tantrism, the second way, which makes coitus a sacrament representing the *unio mystica*.

WHAT IS TANTRISM?

Tantrism is unique among Yoga paths in its fundamental character and in tone. Its goal is that of all the Yogas, but the means is an exuberant 'yes-saying' to the experiences of living. It welcomes the dance of life, whether macabre or joyous, the play of universal energy which, as William Blake said, is eternal delight.

According to Tantric doctrine, human history is divided into four ages, representing a decline from the Golden Age to the Dark Age, which is our own. The *Tantras* (Tantric scriptures) are Siva's answer to the request of Shakti (the Divine Mother) for guidance for our pleasure-loving age (*Kali yuga*). One of the *Tantras* says: 'Eating and coitus are desired and natural to men, and their use is regulated for their benefit in the ordinance of Siva.' Another *Tantra* says: 'She [Shakti] does not exact from her weak and short-lived children of the *Kali yuga* long and trying *Brahmacharya* (celibacy) and austerity to show them the way to her Lotus Feet . . . The low and the high, all are equally taken care of, and for all the path has been made smooth and straighter.'

The word *tantra* derives from a root connected with the interdependence of warp and woof in weaving. The Tantrist does not withdraw from the world but faces, squarely and with heightened perception, its pain and pleasure, suffering and joy, destruction and construction, darkness and light – and, by meditation full of rich and subtle imagery, he transcends the polar opposites.

Tantrism is not, however a licence to 'do what you will' or to indulge in orgies of pleasure; though, inevitably, it has sometimes been taken as such, and the excesses of some sects have given it a bad name with orthodox Hindus and Buddhists. The person who makes Tantric ritual an excuse for licentiousness and who concentrates on the physical pleasure instead of the mystical expansion of consciousness is held by Hindu and Buddhist alike to be a 'fool', for he is creating bad *karma* instead of liberating his spirit. Though sometimes a fool who persists in his folly becomes wise, as William Blake pointed out.

Tantrism requires a long preparatory training and careful initiation. Its character, and the dangers of abuse and misinterpretation, led to its practices becoming closely-guarded secrets. One text puts it: 'Whereas the other scriptures are like a common woman, free to all, the Tantra is like a secret house-bride.'

Tantric texts can be read and interpreted at several levels: physiological, psychological, symbolical, occult, mystical, and so on. This gives them extraordinary depth. Occidental students of Tantrism in the nineteenth century missed the point and saw only raw sex, macabre rites, and a pursuit of magical and occult power; they failed to see the sophistication, subtlety, and spirituality that were there. Today the directness of the language at one level and the nature of the practices no longer shock, as they shocked Christian missionaries and scholars who sprang from a society guilt-ridden about sex.

Tantrism harnesses cosmic energy, which it sees in essence as sexual. Hundreds of years before the birth of Sigmund Freud, Hindu and Buddhist Tantrists were intensely aware of the power of the libido and had worked out ways of ritual and contemplation to channel this force for spiritual ends. Practice (*sadhana*) includes coitus as ritual and contemplation, the coming together of male and female bodies representing the coupling of god and goddess and the union of the great male (positive) and female (negative) polar forces in the cosmos – the energies which the Chinese named *yang* and *yin* respectively. Sexual intercourse thus enacts and represents the *unio mystica* that is the goal of all Yogas.

Tantrism takes its name from the *Tantras*, treatises which instruct in ritual and contemplation. Instructions that could be defined as being of an 'erotic' character make up only six to seven per cent of this literature – most of the passages concern the preparation of ingredients used in ritual, which *mantras* to repeat, the construction of *mandalas*, and so on. The erotic matters are also concerned with ritual and contemplation, including *maithuna* or sacramental coitus. *Saktisangama Tantra* means 'the *Tantra* about Shakti coition' and another text, *kamakalavilasa*, means 'erotic joy in love motion'.

Scholars disagree as to whether Buddhist Tantrism derived from Hindu Tantrism or the reverse. Other scholars say that both originated in a Yogic cult of ancient India, which on meeting with Hindu and Buddhist ideology became Tantric Hinduism and Tantric Buddhism respectively. Both became strong from about the fourth century AD. Tantric Hinduism is strongest in northern India, and Tantric Buddhism in Tibet and Nepal.

'Tantric' can be used as a general term applied to all Yogas using physiological techniques, including Hatha Yoga and Kundalini Yoga.

Tantric Yoga is an at times bizarre but always fascinating mixture of magic, occultism, body and mind mastery, esoteric knowledge, and mysticism of cosmic dimension. It has inspired much exuberant and excellent art and greatly influenced Indian aesthetics. Its insight that the physical union between man and woman in love and mindfulness represents a mystical way is valuable and can be reinterpreted for our age.

SEXUAL AND RELIGIOUS ECSTASY

Philip S. Rawson (52), an authority on Tantric art, has pointed out that 'quick and easy definitions' of Tantrism are impossible, because we are dealing with 'a special manifestation of Indian feeling, art and religion'. Another difficulty is that there is such a variety of belief and practice within Tantrism. 'However,' continues Mr Rawson, 'there is one thread which can guide us through the labyrinth; all the different manifestations of Tantra can be strung on it. This thread is the idea that Tantra is a cult of ecstasy, focused on a vision of cosmic sexuality. Life-styles, ritual, magic, myth, philosophy and a complex of signs and emotive symbols converge upon that vision.'

When Marghanita Laski, in compiling her study of ecstasy, questioned people who had experienced it in their lives, she found that art, nature, and sexual love were the three main triggers, scoring close together. Religion was the next most frequent trigger. In all ecstasies, whatever their cause, the ego sense is weakened and dissolves, and there is a sense of 'homecoming', of finding Reality. There may be physiological concomitants: Miss Laski's ecstatics experienced flashes of light, electrical tinglings in the spine, feelings of inner warmth, and the like (36). Similar sensations are reported by Tantric Yogins.

Sexual love offers the possibility of ecstasy. In this secular age great numbers of men and women make sex a substitute for religion and find in it a way of catching momentarily something of the non-duality, timelessness, and ego-obliteration experienced by the mystics. It is worth pausing to consider how the orgasm blots out both ego and time – two aims of esoteric psychologies. If men and women were granted the experience of orgasm only one or twice in their lives, one could well envisage a world religion being based on it.

Accounts of sexual and of religious ecstasy are unsatisfactory for the same reason: in either case an attempt is being made to describe the ineffable. In accounts of sexual ecstasy mere descriptions of behaviour are obviously inadequate, and the writer must take wing into language that could be applied just as aptly to an account of religious ecstasy. Conversely, descriptions of religious ecstasy often employ language of a sexual character. In particular this is so when religious adoration is operating, focused on a divine figure, as often in Bhakti Hinduism and Christian mysticism.

The ecstasy on the face of St Teresa of Avila (1515-82), as portrayed in white marble by Bernini, could be sexual rather than religious; and she described her visions and raptures in imagery and language so erotic as to embarrass the Church. She had a vision she said, in which an angel appeared carrying a long, golden spear with a fiery tip.

> [He] plunged it into my deepest inward. When he drew it out, I thought my entrails would be drawn out too and when he left me I glowed in the hot fire of love for God. The pain was so strong that I screamed aloud, but simultaneously I felt such infinite sweetness that I wished the pain to last forever. It was the sweetest caressing of the soul by God.

Even so analytical and intellectual a mystic as St John of the Cross evokes the atmosphere of a lovers' tryst in one of his most beautiful poems:

Upon an obscure night
Fevered with Love's anxiety
(O hapless, happy plight!)
I went, none seeing me,
Forth from my house, where all things quiet be.

By night, secure from sight
And by a secret stair, disguisedly,
(O hapless, happy plight!)
By night and privily
Forth from my house, where all things quiet be.

Blest night of wandering
In secret, when by none might I be spied,
Nor do I see anything;
Without a light to guide
Save that which in my heart burnt in my side.

That light did lead me on,
More surely than the shining of noontide
Where well I knew that One
Did for my coming bide;
Where He abode might none but He abide.

O night that didst lead thus,
O night more lovely than the dawn of light;
O night that broughtest us,
Lover to lover's sight,
Lover to loved, in marriage of delight!

Upon my flowery breast
Wholly for Him and Himself for none,
There did I give sweet rest
To my beloved one:
The fanning of the cedars breathed thereon.

(trs. Arthur Symons)

The erotic element in Bhakti Hinduism is direct and unself-conscious. For millions of Indians the love story of Krishna and Rhada embodies Bhakti emotion. Bhakti *kirtans* or song-poems (like this by Vidyapati, translated by A. Coomaraswamy and A. Sen), can be erotic and at the same time exquisite:

She cries: Oh no, no, no! and tears are pouring from her eyes.
She lies outstretched upon the margin of the bed.
His close embrace has not unloosed her zone.
Even of handling her breast has been but little . . .
When Kanu lifts her to his lap, she bends her body back
Like a young snake, untamed by spells.

Vaisnava Sahajayists identify all men with Krishna and all women with Rhada.

GODS AND GODDESSES

It is significant that of the multiplicity of gods and goddesses of Hindusim the most popular has been Krishna. As an *avatar* or earthly incarnation of Vishnu, he pursued erotic adventures that have been a popular subject of Indian literature and art for many centuries.

He was brought up on a cattle farm, where the milkmaids, the wives of the cowherds, all fell in love with him. A popular story culminates in the *Rasa Mandala*, or round dance, in which Krishna dances with all the girls by moonlight, magically providing each cowgirl with a replica of himself, so that each believes she alone danced with him. They throw off their clothes and dance and sing and make love passionately for six months. Finally, they bathe in the Jumna River, and Krishna orders the girls to return to their homes. When they do so, no one is aware that they have not been there all the time.

With characteristic exaggeration, Hindu tradition says there are thirty-three *crores* (a *crore* is ten million) of gods and goddesses. But they are all manifestation of the One, the Absolute, *Brahman*. *Brahman* is not personified, but has a triune manifestation as Brahma the Creator, Vishnu the Preserver, and Siva the Destroyer. Each of these gods has a female helpmate, his *shakti* or earth-power. Hindu sculpture frequently depicts the gods and goddesses engaged in the dance of life or making love.

Indian temple sculpture fascinates and surprises tourists by its erotic exuberance. Piled in tier upon tier in rock recesses, the figures have a unique ripeness and voluptuousness of bodily curve, and their rhythms are those of the dance and sexual love. These male and female figures display all the erotic inventiveness and sportiveness we find in the classic Indian love-manuals, such as the *Kama Sutra* of Vatsayana and the *Ananga Ranga*, both now widely read in the West.

Siva, the Destroyer, also represents the universal force of generation, fertility, and fecundity, destroying only that new life may burgeon. Representations of his *lingam* or phallus are ubiquitous in Hindu temple art. Sometimes *lingam* and *yoni* (vagina) are depicted in union. B. Z. Goldberg (23), in his study of sex in religion, entitled *The Sacred Fire*, says: 'the symbol of the *limgan* is the father of the statue in religious worship'.

The legend behind *lingam* worship is this. Siva's mate had died, and he wandered about the land haggard and disconsolate. The sages who lived in the forest of Daruvanam, shocked to see the god in so piteous a state, saluted him with downcast eyes. But their wives were heartbroken on gazing upon the sad features of Siva and left their husbands to follow the god. Whereupon the sages angrily cursed the god with: 'May his *lingam* fall to the ground!' The curse must have worked, or perhaps Siva decided that, bereaved of his mate, he could dispense with his phallus – whatever way it was, Siva vanished and his *lingam* was found sticking in the ground.

B. Z. Goldberg continues the legend (23):

As the *lingam* fell, it penetrated the lower worlds. Its length increased and its top towered above the heavens. The earth quaked and all there was upon it. The *lingam* became fire and caused conflagration wherever it penetrated. Neither god nor man could find peace or security.

So both Vishnu and Brahma came down to investigate and to save the universe. Brahma ascended to the heavens to ascertain the upper limits of Siva's *lingam*, and Vishnu betook himself to the lower regions to discover its depth. Both returned with the news that the *lingam* was infinite: it was lower than the deep and higher than the heavens.

And the two great gods both paid homage to the *lingam* and advised man to do likewise. They further counselled man to propitiate Parvati, the goddess, that she might receive the *lingam* into her *yoni*.

This was done and the world was saved. Mankind was taught that the *lingam* is not to be cursed or ignored; that it is infinite in its influence for good or evil; and that rather than wishing it destroyed, they should worship it by offering it flowers and perfumes and by burning fires before it.

Whether it was the goddess Venus or the god Siva, whether it was the feminine principle or the masculine, the worship of the god or of the goddess came as a punishment for sex ignored. Love suppressed, offended, and imprisoned came to be rescued by the gods of religion.

Siva's consort or *shakti* turns up variously as Parvati, Durga, Kali, Devi, and Uma. She is the Divine Mother. In Yoga's symbolism the union of Siva and *shakti* represents the mystic union of Self (*Atman*) and Over-Self (*Brahman*).

SACRAMENTAL COITUS

Bearing in mind the unselfconscious erotic element in Hinduism and its history of *lingam* worship and of temple prostitution in which sex was a sacred rite, it need occasion no surprise that schools of Yoga should have developed for which sexual union became a sacrament and a way to illumination.

Sacred prostitution flourished in India for many centuries and continued well into our own. Coupling took place between priest and temple prostitute (*Deva-dasi*) or female visitor, or between prostitute and male visitor. Most of the prostitutes also served as dancing girls and lived within the temple precincts; others lived outside and charged a fee which they passed on to the priests. By initiation the *Deva-dasi* was married to a god, whom she served by dancing and by prostitution. Indian temple harlotry continued into the twentieth century, persisting in some states of South India into the early thirties. Gandhi attacked the practice in 1927 (*Young India*, 6 October 1927, p. 335). The southern state of Travancore, which at the turn of the century had about four hundred *Deva-dasis*, abolished temple prostitution in 1930.

Tantric texts can be read at different levels according to the reader's esoteric knowledge, but statements that *maithuna* (ceremonial intercourse) represents only a symbolic technique and that no actual fleshly union takes place are not in accord with the evidence. While it is true that for some Tantric schools the coincidence of bodies refers to subtle or astral bodies, there can be no denying that within other sects coitus between man and woman in the flesh does occur, with or without orgasm, and that some Tantrists employ actual coitus in the early stages of training until their imaginative and meditative powers have developed enough 'muscle' to enable them to dispense with fleshly union.

Philip Rawson, in the *Catalogue for the Exhibition of Tantric Art Sponsored by the Arts Council of Great Britain* in the autumn of 1971; worte (52):

> Modern writers on Tantra tend to discuss its sexual rituals in an abstract way, as if they were purely imaginary or merely mechanical functions of Yoga. In fact, real intercourse with complete enjoyment can be treated as an icon of what it signifies. . . . The true inner image behind sexual intercourse is a transcendent enjoyment in energetic love-play of the two-sexed divinity in Hinduism or Buddha-nature in Buddhism. The joy of actual sexual intercourse, undertaken in the same spirit as worship of an outer image, can help to awaken in the mind of the *Sadhaka* that permanent inner blissful image, of which human intercourse is another reflection.

Mr Rawson is saying, in effect, that coitus can be a contemplative act, a Yoga – which is what it is in Tantrism. This means that sexual coupling is to be approached with real reverence, the mood is to be built up for days or weeks, and that the union when it comes is not an attempt to extract maximum sensual excitement, but rather a contemplative joy, an *ekstasis*. To ensure this calm centre at the heart of the whirlpool, the couple stay immobile, locked in an embrace; orgasm may or may not be triggered. Such sexual control requires skill in Yogic posturing, breathing and meditation. Coital posture can contribute to stillness: the man sits in one of the traditional cross-legged meditative poses and then the woman sits down on the Yogin's lap with her legs around his waist. The couple then lock in an embrace and stay immobile in a spiritual communion that is given strength and support by their physical union, which is prolonged for many minutes, even several hours, and accompanied by a contemplation that lifts the minds of Yogin and Yogini well above any concern with bodily sensation.

TANTRIC PRACTICE

Tantric meditation is a way of focusing the libido and harnessing its energies for transcendental ecstasy. Yogin and Yogini become god and goddess. The initiation of women for their roles is among the most closely guarded secrets of Tantrism. Those who favour actual rather than imaginative or symbolic intercourse are known as followers of the Left Hand Path. Nothing condemnatory is implied by 'left' – they take their name from the fact that the Yogini at the commencement of the ceremony sits to the left side of the Yogin.

Before one can harness power it is customary first of all to generate it. In Tantric Yoga practice (*sadhana*) the energy and heat is built up in the total organism and is not localized in geneital erethism. Some 'left-hand' sects deliberately flout Brahmin and Buddhist convention and orthodoxy by eating forbidden foods and drinking alcohol. Their five sacraments, known as the five Ms, are eating fish (*matsya*), beef (*mamsa*), and parched grain (*mudra*); drinking alcoholic beverages (*madya*); and ceremonial coitus (*maithuna*). Aphrodisiacs and drugs (mainly *bhang* or *ganjam*, types of cannabis) may be taken. Doubtless a special excitement is engendered through partaking of food and drink normally forbidden.

Mantras – words imbued with sacred, magical, or psychophysiological potency – are repeated, aloud or inwardly. Each Yogi is given a personal *mantra* on initiation into the cult. A *yantra* or mystic diagram is drawn on the ground.

Through meditation, Yogi and Yogini become god and goddess. They participate in ritual purification. Flowers are offered to the 'goddess", who is bathed and anointed with perfumed oils.

Coitus follows, an act of worship and contemplation. The male and female universal principles merge and unite, duality is overcome, the opposites are transcended.

Tantric practice (*sadhana*) is so profuse, complex and varied that it would be impossible to do it justice in the space available in this chapter. Nor does it readily come within our practical approach to Yoga. The ritual is long-drawn-out and makes wearisome reading for those outside the tradition.

SEMEN HOARDING

Sexual energy is at its most intense and explosive at orgasm, yet the Tantrists mostly avoid orgasm in ceremonial coition. One might expect to find in Tantrism a view of orgasm on lines similar to that expounded by Wilhelm Reich, the Austrian psycho-analyst and natural scientists, who saw the orgasm as the answer to man's main health and social problems. The Tantrists have two reasons for avoiding orgasm in *maithuna*.

The first reason is that the energy which normally goes into orgasm is in *maithuna* harnessed for meditative ends. The total effect of the contemplative embrace is one of spiritual communion, sexually sustained at what the sexologists call the plateau phase. Contemplation, which may go on for one or two hours, would be violently disrupted by the orgasm of either partner. And when *maithuna* takes place entirely within consciousness, attaining orgasm would clearly be difficult.

The second reason why the Tantrist may avoid orgasm is to be found in the strong belief that semen is the gross form of a concentrated psychic power called *ojas*, and that by retaining semen (*bindu*) one builds up radiant energy (*tejas*) in the body. Thus one finds either chastity or coitus without ejaculation favoured in Yogic texts. Seminal fluid is precious, and to be hoarded. This concept is widespread in the East, though not supported in any way by medical science.

Magical power has been ascribed to semen from man's earliest history. In Indian folk-lore one finds the superstition that if you cut the skin of one of India's wandering holy men the wound will exude not blood but semen. The legends of the Naths depict woman as a serpent or tigress who steals man's source of life power: his semen. Similar stories are found in the folk tradition of many cultures. There is a belief in Yoga schools that exceptional powers (*siddhis*), such as telepathy and clairvoyance, result from transferring semen or, more strictly speaking, *ojas* to the brain, the eyes, and so on.

There is even a Yogic technique for reabsorbing the ejaculate, which was described in the section on Yogic hygiene in *Yoga and Vitality*. Nothing symbolic is implied here, but an actual muscle control whereby water can be drawn up the urethra and held for a while in the gladder.

A story is told of the fifth Dalai Lama (who died about 1680) which only makes sense if one knows about the Yogic technique of reabsorbing the ejaculate. It appears that the fifth Dalai Lama had a reputation as a womanizer. (He also wrote love songs still popular with the Tibetans.) One day, standing on one of the upper terraces of his palace, the Dalai Lama listened to criticisms of his way of life from his advisers, to which he retorted: 'Yes, it is true that I have women . . . but copulation for me is not the same thing as it is for you.' He then stepped to the edge of the terrace and pissed over it. The urine streamed downwards, from terrace to terrace, until it reached the bottom of the palace. Then, to the great astonishment of onlookers, it began to flow upwards, defying the law of gravity by climbing terrace after terrace, and finally re-entering the Dalai Lama's body at the point of its previous exit. He then turned to his advisers and said: 'Unless you can do the same, you must realize that my sexual relations are different from yours.'

The meaning behind the story lies in the spiritual power ascribed to semen by the Tibetans and the technique whereby the ejaculate can be reabsorbed. The Dalai Lama, it will be noted, was not concerned with the sinfulness of sex or with the risk of making his mistresses pregnant – but he was very much concerned with retaining his semen.

Taoists have used a more mechanical but simpler technique, pressing on the perineum (between scrotum and anus) at the moment of orgasm, and thereby diverting the seminal fluids into the bladder.

Medical knowledge indicates that reabsorbed or diverted semen will pass into the bladder and not the testicles. Yogins reply that even if this is so, the psychic force (*ojas*) will permeate the body.

A persistent superstition, found in many cultures, is that a drop of semen is equal to an ounce of blood. One recalls that less than a hundred years ago European and American doctors were terrifying boys by telling them of the dreadful perils to health and sanity caused by loss of 'vital fluids' through masturbation or 'wet dreams'. This warning is no longer heard. Belief that semen contains concentrated life force or that its loss is debilitating does not now accord with anything known to medical science, though we cannot dismiss it entirely on that account.

KAREZZA

The Tantric practice of prolonged intercourse without orgasm has been followed in many cultures and goes under a variety of names.

A comparable practice among the Bedouins called Udhrism or the cult of Beni Udhra was praised by some Arab poets and spread to Spain and parts of Europe. Men and women embraced either without penetration of the vagina, or with penetration, but without orgasm. The latter control was called *ismak* or 'retention'. The aims of the technique were spiritual bliss and illumination. The cult inspired some intensely erotic and mystical poetry.

In the West the technique has gone under various names, the best known of which are male continence, *coitus reservaturs*, and *karezza*. It has been practised by some mystical or semi-mystical cults. The best known example of male continence is the sect founded by John Humphrey Noyes (died 1886) at Oneida Creek, New York State, in the middle of the last century. At first Noyes advocated 'complex marriage', which meant that the sexes practised a form of free love, which he felt fulfilled biblical teaching. Sexual congress took place, without the male ejaculating. It was known at first as male continence, and later as *coitus reservatus*.

The more sophisiticated name *karezza* or *carezza* (a Persian word) was given to the withholding of orgasm by both partners by Alice Bunker Stockham in her book *Karezza*, published in 1896. Intercourse was sustained for from one to two hours, and the embrace repeatedly taken to the verge of climax. It was claimed for *karezza* that it led to rejuvenation, good health, a feeling of buoyancy and well-being, heightened perception of natural objects and, most important of all, the raising of levels of consciousness.

Karezza was vehemently attacked on moral grounds, and criticized for medical reasons. Prolonged tumescence, doctors said, could lead to inflammation of the genital organs, and psychological damage could result from the unreleased build-up of nervous force. Supporters of *karezza* replied that there were no reported cases of harm on either score: the moral criticisms they countered by saying that *karezza* 'spiritualized' sexual relations.

The sublimation of sexuality for purposes of spiritual illumination by sleeping chastely with virgins was catigated by St Paul in the First Epistle to the Corinthians. A more tolerant account is that by John Cowper Powys in his novel *Weymouth Sands;* in this the eccentric mystic Sylvanus Cobbold sleeps chastely with young girls.

YOGA AND SEXUAL FITNESS

Tantrists are familiar with the muscle contractions and locks, called *mudras* and *bandhas*, which we described in *Yoga and Vitality* as a means of enhancing sexual vigour. These controls, which belong to esoteric Yoga, strengthen and tone the sexual organs, muscles and glands.

It should be noted, too, that the postures (*asanas*) of Hatha Yoga aid sexual fitness in two ways. Firstly, they increase suppleness for what is after all an athletic or gymnastic performance of a kind. Secondly, they promote the health and tone of the spine, nervous system, glands, and vital organs. Blood is carried to the pelvis and feeds the spinal nerves. Such famous poses as the Cobra, Bow, Locust, Spinal Twist, Supine Thunderbolt, Shoulderstand, Spinal Rock, Fish, and Lotus are held by Yogins to enhance sexual health, and the muscle controls *Uddiyana* (Abdominal Retraction) and *Nauli* (Isolation of the Recti) are closely associated with sex fitness.

THE SPIRIT OF TANTRISM

For most readers it is the special spirit or feeling of Tantrism, rather than its complicated ritualistic practices, that will prove valuable. Tantric Yoga is a strange mixture of magical and occult belief and practice, often-macabre rites, bodily and mental mastery, and sexual and mystical wisdom. Disregarding the mumbo-jumbo, its insight that the physical union between partners in love and mindfulness represents a mystical way is valuable, and can be reinterpreted for our times and circumstances in ways productive of human happiness and self-actualization. It heightens our awareness and enjoyment of the present moment, not only in sex but in all of life's activities.

The follower of the Tantric way, says Alan Watts (65),

> discovers that existence is basically a kind of dancing or music – an immensely complex energy pattern which needs no explanation other than itself – just as we do not ask what is the *meaning* of fugues by Bach or sonatas by Mozart. We do not dance to reach a certain point on the floor, but simply to dance. Energy itself, as William Blake said, is eternal delight – and all life is to be lived in the spirit of rapt absorption in an arabesque of rhythms.

The Tantrist worships the female principle, representing the negative, dark, and earthy aspects of the universe, and seeks union with this *shakti*. He accepts darkness with light, light with darkness, realizing that each is necessary to the Whole. Both are present and each leaps to the eye as figure or ground according to which viewpoint one adopts – like those double images that can be either two shaded faces in profile or a white chalice against a dark background. 'Some understanding of Tantra is therefore a marvellous and welcome corrective to certain excesses of Western civilization,' Alan Watts continues:

> We over-accentuate the positive, think of the negative as 'bad', and thus live in a frantic terror of death and extinction which renders us incapable of 'playing' life with an air of noble and joyous detachment. Failing to understand the musical quality of nature, which fulfils itself in an eternal present, we live for a tomorrow which never comes – like an orchestra racing to attain the finale of a symphony. But through understanding the creative power of the female, of the negative, of empty space, and of death, we may at least become completely alive in the present.

XVI Press-button Yoga: Biofeedback

IS BIOFEEDBACK INSTRUMENTAL YOGA?

This chapter deals with Yoga with the aid of electrical equipment – instrumental or press-button Yoga, which is what biofeedback claims to be, and certainly in part is.

The part of biofeedback that corresponds with elements in Yoga is auto-control of the involuntary nervous system, that section responsible for such physiological functions as the heartbeat, blood pressure, and the different kinds of brain waves. This is the kind of body-mind control with which Indian fakirs and Yogins have on occasions surprised observing doctors and scientists. Now, with biofeedback instruments, these startling feats can be learned by most men and women. The mastery extends to producing those brain wave patterns observable in meditating Yogins and Zen monks.

The main feature of the learning process is that the working of functions in the human body hitherto thought involuntary can be translated into some sort of signal, by observing which we can train ourselves to regulate the internal body function. Of biofeedback, two American psychologists (33) have written that 'the ultimate possibilities of man's self-control are nothing less than the evolution of an entirely new culture where people can change their mental and physical states as easily as switching channels on a television set.'

Increasing the state of muscular relaxation, lowering the blood pressure, switching the brain's 'engine' into neutral gear and free-wheeling for a while – all these controls come within the capabilities of the majority of men and women training with biofeedback apparatus. The medical importance is obvious, and the personal importance for the layman is full of fascinating possibilities.

If Yoga is modification of the mind-stuff – Patanjali's classic definition – biofeedback is a kind of Yoga. But as yet there is no substantial evidence of meditators by machine having peak illuminative experiences that transform the personality permanently, which is what Yoga claims for the experience of *samadhi*. In regulating physiological processes hitherto thought inaccessible to direct conscious control, except as displayed occasionally by remarkable Yogins, biofeedback is, again, a kind of Yoga. As an aid to deep relaxation, biofeedback promotes one of Yoga's greatest benefits to harassed Western man.

The number of scientific papers (mostly American) on biofeedback is already considerable. Valuable and startling gains in autocontrol are objectively recorded.

BIOFEEDBACK EXPLAINED

Biofeedback instruments may be intricate, but the principle of feedback is simple enough and in practice known to everyone. Like Molière's M Jourdain, who discovered to his great surprise that he had been speaking prose all his talking life, we find on examination that each of us depends on feedback for learning efficiency in everyday living. The term itself belongs to the early days of radio, but its operation in the human organism belongs to the total history of man.

Say you visit a funfair and decide to try your luck at dislodging coconuts by throwing balls at them. Your first throw misses a coconut by several inches to the right hand side. You now make a mind-body adjustment for the next throw, but you over-compensate so that the ball misses its target by a few inches to the left hand side. The third throw now has a more hopeful chance of success, for past performance – the first two throws – has been imprinted and the information has been processed for the third throw. That is the way efficient motor performance is acquired. As babies we learned to use our hands by watching them, and by trial and error, and we learned to speak on the basis of listening to our first attempts and improving upon them. So we know what feedback means – we have been using it all of our lives.

Biofeedback (the Greek word *bios* means 'life') is a special kind of feedback that is concerned with such life processes as the beating of the heart, the pressure and circulation of the blood, and the energy waves of the brain. Through biofeedback training we develop control over inner physiological functions in the same way as, by feedback learning, we have developed manual and other human skills which we use to survive in a complex and hazardous environment. Every animal owes its performance and survival to feedback.

The reason why biofeedback training is an exciting new advance is that modern technology offers us the opportunity to become aware of inner functioning by translating it into an outward signal – visual (a flashing light, a moving needle, oscillating pens on a graph) or aural (a sustained tone, 'bleeps' or clicks, amplified breathing or heartbeats). The translated signals open up new territories of self-regulation. We tune into physiological processes we had thought involuntary and beyond conscious direction. The senses of sight and hearing which all our lives we have been accustomed to use to guide our movements, are now employed for monitoring the functioning of our inner organs. We raise or lower the pitch of a tone or take note of what subtleties of sensation accompany a 'bleep', and in doing so are able to regulate normally involuntary physiological mechanisms. We learn, as one American psychologist put it, 'to play our internal organs'. Yogins sometimes achieve this tuning in without the aid of electrical instruments; but few of us can develop such sensitivity of awareness that, without assistance, we can listen to the circulation of the blood and to other internal bodily activities normally outside the reach of conscious attention. Biofeedback equipment provides that assistance.

THE TWO NERVOUS SYSTEMS

The two nervous systems are the voluntary and the involuntary systems. The voluntary system gives us control over the nerves responsible for movements of the skeletal muscles, that is, for deliberate body movements. The involuntary or autonomic nervous system controls the functions of the heart, glands, and digestion, and controls temperature adjustment – physiological processes that normally can be allowed to get on with their vital work without interference, interruption, or direction from consciousness. Yet when something goes wrong with these processes it can clearly be of value if the person concerned is able to regulate his inner functioning to the benefit of his health and efficiency.

In *Yoga and Vitality* we described the Yogic technique of *tumo*, by which heat can be engendered in any part of the body – say a foot or a hand — by directing consciousness to that place. Biofeedback equipment brings *tumo*, which the Yogi takes months, even years, to master, within the reach of the majority of users in a matter of hours.

Professor Neal E. Miller (14), of Rockefeller University, New York, taught rats whose voluntary nervous systems had been paralysed by curare to gain mastery over their involuntary nervous systems. One of his rats learned to blush one ear at a time. Yet Professor Miller had great difficulty in finding people to work with him on experiments based on what seemed too far-fetched a possibility.

BIOFEEDBACK THERAPY

The areas of medical treatment in which biofeedback has been found helpful are cases of migraine and tension headaches, high blood pressure, heart trouble, insomnia, muscular tics, and anxiety.

At a number of hospitals and medical schools in America patients have been taught to monitor and regulate their heartbeats, an ability retained outside the laboratory. The importance of such a skill in cases of heart disease and irregularity is obvious.

Biofeedback training opens up many possibilities of auto-healing. However, attempts at self-cure should not be taken beyond relaxation to tampering with the functioning of vital organs and processes without prior medical consultation. This is an area in which to 'go it alone' could be highly dangerous.

REDUCING ANXIETY

Dr Paul Grim (25) has achieved rapid results in reducing anxiety by using respiration biofeedback. The subjects were ninety-five nursing students. A psychological test prior to relaxation was used to determine their general level of anxiety. The students then were taught to let go from tension by listening to their amplified breathing while lying limp on the bed. Following the period of training in relaxation, the psychological test measuring anxiety was taken again by each subject. The result? A significant reduction of the level of anxiety. Listening to the amplified breathing led to respiration becoming smoother and more rhythmic – exactly what happens in Yogic *pranayama* (breath control), which also induces relaxation. Amplifying the sound of breathing could be an aid to making rapid progress in some aspects of *pranayama*. A similar monitoring effect can be obtained in two ways without electrical apparatus – by covering the ears with the hands, and by lying back in the bath so that the water covers the ears but the nose is held out of the water. Awareness of emptying and filling the lungs with air is popular as a meditative practice in Buddhism and in some schools of Yoga.

Other biofeedback methods aim at relaxing the forehead muscles, which are intimately linked with anxiety. Electrodes pick up any movement of the fontalis muscle, and this is fed into an EMG (electromyograph) machine. The signal is a tone which rises when the muscle contracts and falls when it relaxes. This and related equipment is available to the general public as well as to clinicians. One can learn to recognize subtle rises in tension that normally escape awareness, and to let go from them.

But the biofeedback method of dissolving anxiety and inducing mental calm which most interests us here is that which produces alpha electrical activity in the brain. This is the activity found in meditating Yogins.

BRAIN WAVES

Hans Berger, a German scientist, discovered the presence of brain waves shortly after the First World War. In July 1924 he attached two electrodes from a galvanometer to the scalp of a seventeen-year-old mental patient and found that the brain emits a form of electrical energy. During the following five years Berger established the existence of two distinct brain wave patterns, which he named 'alpha' and 'beta'. He saw that beta registered during concentrated mental work, whereas alpha was associated with a relaxed passive state. Berger was dismissed in 1938 by the Nazis from his position at the University of Jena, and committed suicide three years later.

The modern EEG machine (electroencephalograph) records brain wave patterns by means of a row of oscillating inked pens 'writing' on a continuously winding roll of graph paper.

Beta brain wave, with a frequency of over 14 cycles per second, is the commonest pattern in active minds. It is produced in mental work, such as adding up figures or solving a crossword puzzle. Beta rhythms are marked by much electrical static.

Alpha activity has a frequency of 8-13 cycles per second, with associated feelings of passivity. Not everyone finds the sensation pleasant, but most people do. The mind in the alpha state is neither active nor drowsy, but in neutral. When the brain rhythms of meditating Yogins were tested with EEG equipment, alpha patterns were recorded. For reasons not yet understood, a few people produce alpha patterns almost all the time, and some others cannot produce them at all.

Since Berger's time two more electrical brain patterns have been found, and named 'delta' and 'theta'.

Theta waves have a frequency of 4-7 cycles per second. This is a rhythm characteristic of the period just before the onset of sleep. Delta waves, with a frequency of ½-6 cycles per second, are rarely found except in sleep.

An intriguing feature of brain wave activity is that at any moment one pattern may be observable in one part of the brain, while a different pattern is observable in another part of the brain. It is usually alpha and beta that are thus simultaneously engaged, and they may suddenly reverse locations. Alpha rhythm is recorded at its intensest at the back of the head, though the wave usually sweeps from the front to the back of the cortex.

CONTROLLING BRAIN RHYTHMS

The discovery of self-regulation of brain waves is accredited to Dr Joe Kamiya (32), who was researching sleep at the University of Chicago in 1958. 'I became fascinated by the alpha rhythm that came and went in the waking EEGs and wondered if, through laboratory experiments with this easily traced rhythm, a subject could be taught awareness of an internal state,' he was to recall. A subject was placed in a darkened room and Dr Kamiya observed the brain wave rhythms on an EEG machine. At various intervals a bell was rung. The subject had to say whether alpha rhythm was present or not. 'The first day, he was right only about 50 per cent of the time, no better than chance. The second day he was right 65 per cent of the time; the third day, 85 per cent. By the fourth day, he guessed right on every trial – 400 times in a row.' Dr Kamiya had an additional surprise with further subjects. 'They were able to control their minds to the extent to entering and sustaining either [alpha or beta] state upon our command.'

From this initial experiment Dr Kamiya went on to using biofeedback for speedier learning of brain wave identification. In his procedure, each time a subject produced alpha waves an auditory signal, a tone, was sustained, cutting off when the brain changed from alpha activity. This kind of training procedure has been followed since, and it normally takes only a few hours to master the technique and produce alpha waves at will. Dr Kamiya observed: 'I generally tend to have more positive liking for the individual who subsequently turns out to learn alpha control more readily.' Other investigators have trained subjects to produce beta, theta, and delta to order.

Some people experience a strange apprehension on changing from beta to alpha activity. They are usually people who like to be 'on the go' all the time, who find it positively uncomfortable to relax and just let the brain 'tick over' for a while. But most people find that alpha rhythm soothes the nervous system. Why listening to or seeing a signal representing brain wave activity should give us power to control consciousness remains a mystery.

Tremors of the eyelids cause bursts of alpha activity in the brain. Two other findings are of interest to the student of Yoga: alpha waves may be produced by holding the breath (as in pranayama), and by looking steadily at some object (as in *trataka*).

BIOFEEDBACK AND MEDITATION

When the brain wave patterns of meditating Yogins have been recorded, alpha rhythms have invariably been observed. Zen monks also showed alpha activity, but some went into the theta wave state. Two Japanese researchers, Akira Kasamatsu and Tomio Hirai (1966), of Tokyo University, studied the brain wave patterns of Zen meditators, and discerned four distinct stages in their meditation.

i The appearance of alpha, even though the meditator's eyes were open

ii An increase in alpha amplitude

iii A decrease of alpha frequency

iv The appearance of a 'rhythmical theta train'. The fourth state is that preceding the onset of sleep – those pre-sleep minutes which are often productive of ideas for writers, composers, artists, and other creative people.

Green, Green, and Walters (1970) found (24) that some of their most relaxed subjects produced theta waves accompanied by dreamlike imagery, and in some cases by the emergence of the deeply-buried contents of the unconscious.

Another study (Anand, 1961) found that the people who normally produce a well-defined alpha pattern are those with the greatest enthusiasm for taking up meditation, and that they show marked ability in the practice.

Researcher Dr Johann Stoyva says that the 'blank mind' state of Zen and Yoga may, with biofeedback procedure, be reached in 'months or even weeks'. Dr Kamiya (the man who discovered that electrical brain patterns could be changed by conscious control), thinks that alpha rhythms are but one factor in meditation, but that the missing factors can be discovered. 'I do think . . . it will be possible to find the unique neurophysiological signature of meditation by checking out other channels – besides alpha. Once we have the complete physiological pattern that characterises meditation, there's no reason why we can't train people, with feedback, to mimic it in a relatively short space of time,' he says.

But would 'the complete physiological pattern' of meditation be identical with the experience of meditation as found in Yoga or Zen? There are many people who doubt it. They also doubt whether *samadhi* or *satori* could ever be duplicated by putting chemicals into the bloodstream or by inducing neurophysiological responses with electrical instruments. The real test will be whether these 'reproduction' peak illuminative experiences of Yoga and Zen will transform the personality totally and lastingly. A few subjects in biofeedback investigation have reported that alpha activity produced states of consciousness superior to those produced by drugs, with the additional advantages of self-control throughout the experiment and no hangovers subsequently.

Mystical illumination is a rare enough experience within the traditional oriental psychologies, and it may be argued that acquiring some of the practical benefits of meditation rapidly by biofeedback makes it of value. Further: this is a push-button age, and many people who feel at home in it will be encouraged to start meditating through the appeal of biofeedback. Dr Eleanor Criswell, director of the Humanistic Psychology Institute, says: 'It has been said that Americans need gadgets in order to be able to do things, so if this is America's gadget way of giving itself permission to meditate, then it's worth it.'

BRINGING TOGETHER THE TWO PSYCHOLOGIES

The scientific method of testing, observing, recording, and presenting the recorded data in papers for scientific journals has been made applicable to psychology by limiting study to observable behaviour. As a result, psychologists split into two camps: behaviourists following investigations by the respected scientific method, and others willing to study and speculate about states of consciousness. Biofeedback studies and controls states of consciousness in a scientific manner, and so helps to draw together the two schools of approach to psychological study and experiment.

BIOFEEDBACK INSTRUMENTS

We conclude this section on biofeedback by indicating the kinds of equipment that are available for home use. Compact, battery-operated instruments are produced for the general public. The following are sold in America and Britain:

i. The EEG machine for regulating brain waves. Electrodes on the scalp pick up and amplify signals from the brain, in particular those with the frequency range known as alpha, each peak of which produces a 'beep' from the instrument's loudspeaker. The user learns when he is producing alpha waves. The concomitant mental state is one of neutral-gear coasting, distinct from concentration, drowsiness, or trance. Alpha is a feature – though not the whole story – of oriental-style meditation.

For reasons not fully understood, some people cannot produce alpha waves and others do so almost all the time. The manufacturers make a part refund to such customers.

ii The EMG (electromyographic) machine, used to gain mastery over physiological processes normally involuntary. Trade name

'Myophone'. It has medical uses, but should not become a substitute for a doctor's care.

iii The GSR (galvanic skin response) machine, which operates by producing a continuous tone. This rises if the user becomes tense or excited in any way. The pitch of the tone drops as relaxation increases. The electrodes are placed on the user's fingertips, and measure the electrical resistance of the skin, which lowers when tension or excitement causes changes in the sweat glands. Conversely relaxation raises skin resistance.

Galvanic skin response provides a rapid method of training a person to recognize both tension and relaxation in the body – the the latter a 'letting go' from the former. Skill in relaxation benefits health, conserves energy, and increases efficiency in work, creativity, and play.

XVII The Future of Yoga

EAST AND WEST – A NEW SYNTHESIS

Interest in Yoga and other Eastern esoteric psychologies has never been so great in the Western world as now – not only among the general public seeking mental energy, peace of mind, and Self-realization, but also among psychologists, psychiatrists, neurologists, and other specialists. This interest marks a slackening, at least among some sections of Western society, of what has been the predominant orientation of occidental civilization for many centuries. The direction of Western civilization has been towards outward achievement, dissecting, classifying, building, producing – and also, indisputably, towards killing, destroying, self-aggrandizement, greed for material possessions and a ruthless competitiveness.

The history of Western Man has been one of conquering nature. He has sought for the meaning of life outside of human consciousness. In contrast, the Eastern truth-seeker has looked within himself. He has sought to learn the secret of nature (the Tao) not by dissecting or conquering it but by recognizing that he is part of the Whole, the One of the mystics.

There is now widespread acknowledgment in both East and West that these contrasting directions of development have been lopsided and harmful.

Eastern religions and philosophies have been criticized, notably by Albert Schweitzer, as life-negating. The measure of truth in this criticism was then accepted by Swami Vivekananda, Rabindranath Tagore, Mahatma Ghandi, and other Indian reformers, and is now widely accepted. Yoga meditation *can* be escapist and world-renouncing; but it is not so in its modern presentation.

Just as the life-negating, passive, and other-worldly side of Eastern thought is being recognized and countered, so, too, occidentals are increasingly aware of the need to counterbalance Western self-aggrandizement, materialism, and compulsive busyness. Among the young there is a spiritual quest that is universalist in outlook and transcends the worn-out dogmas, doctrinal rigidities, and shibboleths of the traditional institutionalized religions. One aspect of the Western counterbalancing is the growing interest in Eastern methods of relaxation and meditation. Meditation is a degree subject at some American universities. Meditation centres are a feature of many European and American cities. Meditation is taught to air pilots, to hospital patients, to business executives, to factory workers, and to schoolchildren to reduce stress and to improve psycho-physical efficiency.

There are many signs of a new synthesis of Eastern and Western attitudes, ideas, and techniques of self-development. In terms of recent scientific research into the workings of the brain, this represents a harmonizing of the functioning of the right and left hemispheres, and in psychological terms the production of spiritual ambiverts instead of introverts and extraverts.

SCIENCE LOOKS AT YOGA

'There is a new conception of man's capacities forming within the scientific community,' says Dr James Fadiman of Stanford University. 'During the twentieth century academic science has radically underestimated man – his sensitivity to subtle source of energy, his capacity for love, understanding and transcendence, his self-control.'

The new approach is marked by less rigidity in drawing specialist boundaries and a zestful exploration of fields of inquiry hitherto labelled 'fringe science'. Biofeedback is one of the new developments and there are many others.

The new intellectual adventurousness is revealed by some of the contents of college and university curricula and the text-books that go with them. A book of readings called *The Nature of Human Consciousness* (48) includes papers drawn from scientific, medical, psychiatric, and psychological journals on, to mention a few titles, 'Bimodal Consciousness', 'Deautomatization and the Mystic Experience', 'The Physiology of Meditation', and Electroencephalographic Study on the Zen Meditation (Zazen),' and 'Implications of Physiological Feedback Training'. There are also extracts from books on Yoga, Zen, Sufism, and the *I Ching*.

Laboratory tests have been carried out on meditating Yogins in India, Zen monks in Japan, and Transcendental Meditators in America. Consciousness is being studied from new angles and in new ways, and Yoga is being subjected to scientific examination. Most leading Yoga Masters welcome the new studies. Yoga will benefit from losing any superstitious accretions. Out of the scientific investigation should come a clearer understanding of what is valuable in Yogic techniques. It should lead to old methods being streamlined and freshened up and to new methods being introduced.

THE EVOLUTION OF HUMAN CONSCIOUSNESS

An East-West synthesis harbours much that is valuable for the psychological development and future history of mankind.

In his introduction to his translation of the *Brahma Sutra*, S. Radhakrishnan, a great Indian philosopher and a President of India, wrote (51):

> Man's quest for perfection consists in organizing the things of body, mind and soul into a whole. The activities of the human spirit are interrelated, the artistic and the ethical, the religious and the rational. Man is a miniature of the universe in which he lives. Man, as he is, is a transitional being, an unfinished experiment. When he is awakened, he is at peace with himself, he thinks and acts in a new way. For this awakening, man has to take another step in his evolution.

In any step upward on the evolutionary ladder, the Yoga of Meditation is likely to have a major role to play.

Glossary of Sanskrit Terms

Abhyasa Yoga – Yoga of Steady Effort
Acharya – religious teacher
Advaita Vedanta – branch of the Vedanta philosophy whose central tenet is non-duality
Aham Brahma asmi – I am Brahman
Ahamkara – the 'I'-sense
Ahimsa – non-violence
Ajna chakra – brow centre
Anahata chakra – heart centre
Anga – limb; Patanjali lists eight *angas* of Yoga
Antaranga – the three internal practices of meditation
Apara – lower
Aparigraha – non-possessiveness
Asamprajnata samadhi – unconscious *samadhi*
Asanas – bodily postures
Ashram – Yoga centre or school
Asmita – the sense of I-am-ness
Asramas – stages of life for the Hindu
Asteya – non-stealing
Atman – the Self
Atman Yoga – Yoga of Self
AUM – see OM
Avatar – earthly incarnation of a divinity
Avidya – metaphysical ignorance
Bandha – muscular lock; binding
Bhakti Yoga – Yoga of Devotion
Bija – seed
Bindu – point; semen; seed
Brahmacharya – continence
Brahman – the Absolute; the One; Ultimate Reality; Universal Spirit
Brahmins – the highest, priestly caste
Buddhi – intellect; widsom
Buddhi Yoga – Yoga of Wisdom
Chakra – an energy centre in the subtle body; literally, a vortex
Chela – a pupil
Cit – pure consciousness

Citta – mind-stuff
Crore – ten million
Darshama – viewpoint or vision
Deva-dasi – temple prostitute
Dharana – concentration; holding the attention steadily on an object
Dharma – way of life; civilization; national consciousness
Dhyana – contemplation; the free-flowing continuation of *dharana*
Dhyana Yoga – Yoga of Meditation
Drashta or *drashtri* – the Seer, Witness, or Looker
Ekagra – one-pointed; concentrated
Ekamevadvitiyam – one without a second
Gunas – the three inherent qualities of Nature
Guru – teacher
Hatha Yoga – Yoga of Bodily Control
Ida – left nerve channel of the subtle body
Isvara or *Ishvara* – Supreme Being; God
Japa – repetition of a *mantra*
Jivatma or *Jivatman* – the individual soul
Jnana Yoga – Yoga of Self-knowledge
Jyotir or *tajo dhyana* – luminous contemplation
Kaivalya – absolute independence and freedom
Kali yuga – our pleasure-loving age
Karma – action; the law of cosmic cause and effect
Karma Yoga – Yoga of Action
Klesas – afflictions; suffering
Kshatriyas– the caste of princes, aristocrats and warriors
Kundalini – serpent power; latent energy at the base of the spine
Lingam – phallus
Mahat – cosmic consciousness
Maithuna – sacramental coitus, representing the *unio mystica*
Manas – mind
Mandala – circle; the most important oriental symbol for unity and wholeness
Manipura chakra – solar plexus centre
Mantra – a sound-symbol; incantation
Maya – illusion; the illusory world
Mimansa – one of the six schools of Indian philosophy
Moksha or *mukti* – liberation; spiritual freedom
Mudra – a muscular contraction
Mukti – see *moksha*
Muladhara chakra – root centre
Nada – internal sound
Nadi – a channel of the subtle body
Naishkaramya karma – actionless action
Nauli – isolation of the recti muscles in the central abdomen
Nirbija samadhi – *samadhi* without seed
Nirodhah – restraint
Nirvicara – a grade of *samprajnata samadhi*
Nirvitarka – a grade of *samprajnata samadhi*

Niyamas – observances
Nyaya – one of the six schools of Indian philosophy
Ojas – concentrated psychic power
OM (AUM) – sacred syllable representing the Absolute; the chief *mantra*
Pada – part of a book
Padmasana – Lotus Posture
Para – higher
Pingala – right nerve channel of the subtle body
Prakriti – eternal Nature; basic substance; the Uncaused Cause
Prana – cosmic energy; life force; breath of life
Pranava – OM, representing the Absolute
Pranayama – breath control
Pratyahara – sense withdrawal; turning the attention inwards
Purusha – soul; pure consciousness
Raja Yoga – Yoga of Mental Mastery
Rajas – one of the three *gunas*; activity; energy; the kinetic principle
Sabija samadhi – *samadhi* with seed
Sadhaka – a seeker or aspirant
Sadhana – practice
Sahasrara chakra – crown of the head centre
Samadhi – the highest stage of Yoga meditation; Self-realization; Absorption
Samkhya – one of the six schools of Indian philosophy
Samkhya Yoga – Yoga of Science; literally, number
Samprajnata samadhi – conscious *samadhi*
Samskaras – mental impressions
Samyama – the final three stages of meditation taken together: *dharana*, *dhyana* and *samadhi*
Sannyasa Yoga – Yoga of Renunciation
Sannyasi – one who has renounced the world
Santosha – contentment
Sat chit ananda – bliss consciousness; literally, being-consciousness-bliss
Sattva – the finest of the three *gunas*; purity; intelligence; orderliness; illumin ation
Satya – truthfulness
Saucha – purity
Savicara – a grade of *samprajnata samadhi*
Savitarka – a grade of *samprajnata samadhi*
Shakti – female creative power; earth power; goddess
Siddhasana – Perfect Posture or Adept's Posture
Siddhi – psychic attainment or power
Sthiti – state
Sthula dhyana – gross contemplation, with form
Sudras – the caste of servants and labourers
Sukhasana – Easy Posture
Sukshma sharira – the subtle or astral body
Suksma dhyana – subtle contemplation
Sushumna – central channel carrying *kundalini* energy
Sutra – thread; highly condensed, aphoristic method of literary expression

Svadhyaya – study
Swadhisthana chakra – pelvic centre
Tajo dhyana – see *jyotir dhyana*
Tamas – one of the three *gunas*; inertia; mass; resistance; stability; solidity; durability
Tanmatras – the five potentials of matter: light, sound, smell, taste, and touch
Tantras – treatises of the Tantric schools
Tantric Yoga – Yoga practice based on physiological disciplines
Tapas – austerity
Tat tvam asi – 'That thou art'
Tattwas – the categories or thatnesses, of which there are twenty-four
Tejas – radiant energy
Trataka – gazing steadily at an object; one of the six purifying processes of Hatha Yoga
Uddiyana – retraction of the abdomen
Vairagya – non-attachment; literally, uncolouredness
Vaisesika – one of the six schools of Indian philosophy
Vaisyas – the caste of merchants, farmers, and professional people
Vedanta – one of the six schools of Indian philosophy; literally, the end of the *vedas*
Vibhuti – divine power
Vijnana Yoga – Yoga of Comprehension
Vishudda Chakra – throat centre
Vritti – literally, whirlpool; agitation in the mind-stuff
Yamas – abstinences
Yantra – a form or design symbol
Yoga – Union; mystical Absorption; *Atman* and *Brahman* known as One; literally, to yoke, to join; one of the six schools of Indian philosophy
Yoni – vagina

Bibliography

1. Ashe, Geoffrey, *The Art of Writing Made Simple*, W. H. Allen, 1972.
2. Baker, Father Augustin, *Holy Wisdom, or Directions for the Prayer of Contemplation*, Burns, Oates & Washbourne, 1876.
3. Barnes, Hazel E., *Sartre*, J. B. Lippincott Co., New York, 1973; Quartet Books, London, 1974.
4. Baudouin, Charles, *Suggestion and Auto-suggestion*, Dodd, Mead & Co., New York, 1922, Allen & Unwin, 1949.
5. Behanan Kovoor T., *Yoga: A Scientific Evaluation*, The Macmillan Co., New York, 1937; Dover Publications, New York, 1959.
6. Bouquet, A. C., (ed.) *Sacred Books of the World*, Penguin Books, 1954.
7. Brunton, Paul, *A Search in Secret India*, Rider & Co., 1934.
8. Brunton, Paul, *The Quest of the Overself*, Rider & Co., 1937.
9. Danielou, Alain, *Yoga: The Method of Reintegration*, Johnson Publications, 1949, University Books, New York, 1949.
10. De, Sushil Kumar, 'The Bhakti-Rasa-Sastra of Bengal Vaishnavism', *Indian Historical Quarterly* (Calcutta), viii, 4 (1932)
11. Deikman, Arthur J., 'Implications of Experimentally Induced Contemplative Meditation', *Journal of Nervous and Mental Disease*, 142, No. 2, 101-16.
12. Deikman, Arthur J., 'Meditation and the Mystic Experience', *Psychiatry*, 29 (1966), 324-38. Included in Robert E. Ornstein (ed.) *The Nature of Human Consciousness*, W. H. Freeman & Co., San Francisco, 1973.
13. Deussen, P., *Outlines of Indian Philosophy*, Carl Curtus, Berlin, 1907.
14. Di Cara, L., and N. Miller, 'Instrumental Learning of Vasomotor Responses by Rats: learning to respond differentially in the ears', *Science*, 159 (1968), 1485-6.
15. Dvivedi, Manilal Nabhubhai (tr.), *The Yoga Sutras of Patanjali*, 1890. Madras.
16. Ebdon, Martin (ed.), *Maharishi, The Guru: An International Symposium*, New American Library, New York, 1968.
17. Eliade, Mircea, *Images and Symbols*, Paris, 1952; Harvill Press, 1961.
18. Eliade, Mircea, *Yoga: Immortality and Freedom*, Routledge & Kegan Paul, 1958.
19. Evans-Wentz, W. Y. (ed)., *The Tibetan Book of the Dead*, Oxford University Press, 1927.
20. Freuchen, Peter, *The Book of the Eskimos*, Fawcett World Library, New York, 1959.

21. Furlong, Monica, *Contemplating Now*, Hodder & Stoughton, 1971.
22. Garbe, Richard von, *Philosophy of Ancient India*, The Open Court Publishing Co., Chicago, 1897.
23. Goldberg, B. Z., *The Sacred Fire : the Story of Sex in Religion*, Grove Press, New York, 1958.
24. Green, E., A. Green and E. Walters, 'Voluntary Control of Internal States', *Psychological and Physiological Journal of Transpersonal Psychology* 2, No. 1 (1970), 1-26.
25. Grim, Paul, 'Anxiety changes produced by self-induced muscular tension and by relaxation with respiration feedback', *Behavior Therapy*, 12 (1971), 11-17.
26. Happold, F. C., *Mysticism : A Study and An Anthology*, Penguin Books, 1963.
27. Jaffe, Aniela in *Man And His Symbols*, by C. G. Jung, Aldus Books 1964.
28. James, William, *On Vital Reserves*, Henry Holt & Co., New York, 1911.
29. James, William, *Varieties of Religious Experience*, Longmans, Green & Co., New York and London, 1902.
30. John of the Cross, St., *The Complete Works of St. John of the Cross*, Newman Press 1953.
31. Kafka, Franz, *The Diaries of Franz Kafka* (1914-23), Martin Secker & Warburg, 1949.
32. Kamiya, Joe, 'Conscious control of brain waves', *Psychology Today* 1, (1968), 57-60.
33. Karlins, Marvin and Lewis M. Andrews, *Biofeedback : Turning on the Power of Your Mind*, Garnstone Press, 1973.
34. Koestler, Arthur, *The Lotus and the Robot*, Hutchinson, 1966.
35. Krishna, Gopi, *The Secret of Yoga*, Harper & Row, New York, 1972; Turnstone Books, London, 1973.
36. Laski, Marghanita, *Ecstasy, A Study of Some Secular and Religious Experiences*, Cresset Press, 1961.
37. Linssen, Robert, *Zen : The Art of Life*, Pyramid Communications, New York, 1972.
38. Luk, Charles (Lu k'uan Yu), *The Secrets of Chinese Meditation*, Rider & Co., 1964.
39. Lysebeth, Andre van, *Yoga Self-taught*, Allen & Unwin, 1971
40. Mahesh Yogi, Maharishi, *On the Bhagavad Gita*, SRM Publications, 1967; Penguin Books, 1969.
41. Mahesh Yogi, Maharishi, *The Science of Being and the Art of Living*, SRM Publications, 1963.
42. Mann, W. Edward, *Orgone, Reich and Eros*, Simon & Schuster, New York, 1973.
43. Mascaro, Juan (tr.), *The Upanishads*, Penguin Books, 1965.
44. Menen, Aubrey, *The New Mystics*, Thames & Hudson, 1974.
45. Menen, Aubrey, *The Space Within the Heart*, Hamish Hamilton, 1970.
46. Naranjo, Claudio and Robert E. Ornstein, *On the Psychology of Meditation*, The Viking Press, New York, 1971.
47. Ornstein, Robert E., *The Psychology of Consciousness*, W. H. Freeman & Co., San Francisco, 1972.
48. Ornstein, Robert E. (ed.), *The Nature of Human Consciousness : A Book of*

Readings, W. H. Freeman & Co., San Francisco, 1973.
49. Prabhupada Swami A. C. Bhaktivedanta *Our Real Life*, the Krishna Consciousness Movement, N. D.
50. Radhakrishnan, S., *The Hindu View of Life*, Allen & Unwin, 1927.
51. Radhakrishnan, S. (tr.), *The Brahma Sutra*, Allen & Unwin, 1960.
52. Rawson, Philip S., *Catalogue of the Exhibition of Tantric Art Sponsored by the Arts Council of Great Britain*, 1971.
53. Rele, Vansant, *The Mysterious Kundalini*. Taraporevala, Bombay, 1927.
54. Sastri, A. Mahadeva (tr.) *The Bhagavad Gita*, with the commentary of Sri Sankaracharya, Mysore, second edition, 1901.
55. Sen, K. M., *Hinduism*, Penguin Books, 1961.
56. Shah, Idries, *The Sufis*, Doubleday & Company, New York, 1964.
57. Sinh, Pancham (tr.), *Hatha Yoga Pradipika*, Lalil Mohan Basu, The Panini Office, Allahabad, 1915.
58. Spiegelberg, Frederick, *Spiritual Practices of India*, Citadel Press, New York, 1962.
59. Suzuki, D. T., *Essays in Zen Buddhism*, Luzac & Co., 1927; Rider & Co., 1949.
60. Taimini, I. K., *The Science of Yoga*, The Theosophical Publishing House, Wheaton, Illinois, 1967.
61. Vasu, Sris Chandra (tr.), *Gheranda Samhita*, Adyar, Madras, 1933.
62. Vidyarnava, Rai Bahadur Srisa Chandra (tr.), *Siva Samhita*, Sudhindra Nath Basu, The Panini Office, Allahabad, 1923.
63. Vishnudevananda, Swami, *The Complete Illustrated Book of Yoga*, Julian Press, New York, 1960; Souvenir Press, London, 1961.
64. Vivekananda, Swami, *Raja Yoga: The Yoga of Conquering Internal Nature*, Advaita Ashrama, Calcutta, 1901.
65. Watts, Alan, *Cloud Hidden, Whereabouts Unknown: A Mountain Journal*, Jonathan Cape, 1974.
66. Werner, H. *Comparative Psychology of Mental Development*, International Universities Press, 1957.
67. Wood, Ernest, *Yoga*, Penguin Books Ltd., 1959.
68. Yasutani Roshi, quoted by Philip Kapleau in *The Three Pillars of Zen*, Beacon Press, Boston, 1967.